W9-CGY-060

DEATH AND LOVE IN THE HOLOCAUST

THE STORY OF SONJA AND KURT MESSERSCHMIDT

DEATH AND LOVE
IN THE HOLOCAUST
THE STORY OF SONJA AND KURT MESSERSCHMIDT

STEVE HOCHSTADT

Boston
2021

Library of Congress Cataloging-in-Publication Data

Names: Hochstadt, Steve, 1948-
Title: Death and love in the Holocaust: the story of Sonja and Kurt Messerschmidt / Steve Hochstadt.
Other titles: Story of Sonja and Kurt Messerschmidt
Description: Brookline, MA: Academic Studies Press, 2022. | Includes bibliographical references and index.
Identifiers: LCCN 2021022438 (print) | LCCN 2021022439 (ebook) | ISBN 9781644696934 (hardback) | ISBN 9781644696941 (paperback) | ISBN 9781644696958 (adobe pdf) | ISBN 9781644696965 (epub)
Subjects: LCSH: Messerschmidt, Kurt, 1915- | Messerschmidt, Sonja, 1925-2010. | Holocaust, Jewish (1939-1945)--Germany. | World War, 1939-1945--Prisoners and prisons, German. | Auschwitz (Concentration camp) | World War, 1939-1945--Prisoners and prisons, German. | Jews--Germany--Berlin--Biography. | Berlin (Germany)--Biography. | CYAC: Holocaust survivors--Biography.
Classification: LCC DS134.4.M48 H63 2022 (print) | LCC DS134.4.M48 (ebook) | DDC 940.53/180922--dc23
LC record available at https://lccn.loc.gov/2021022438
LC ebook record available at https://lccn.loc.gov/2021022439

Copyright © Academic Studies Press, 2022

ISBN 9781644696934 (hardback)
ISBN 9781644696941 (paperback)
ISBN 9781644696958 (adobe pdf)
ISBN 9781644696965 (epub)

Book design by PHi Business Solutions
Cover design by Ivan Grave

Published by Cherry Orchard Books, an imprint of Academic Studies Press
1577 Beacon Street
Brookline, MA 02446, USA

press@academicstudiespress.com
www.academicstudiespress.com

Contents

This work is dedicated to Sonja Kolbelsky Messerschmidt (1925–2010)
and Kurt Messerschmidt (1915–2017)

Illustrations

PHOTOS *

MAP

* All photographs courtesy of the Messerschmidt family.

Acknowledgments

This is a space to show how many people collaborate in order to create a book.

At the head of the line are Sonja and Kurt Messerschmidt. Telling us these stories about their own lives, answering our naive questions, reliving unforgettable fears and humiliations, was their act of love for all of us, who need to know. They were among the first volunteers to be interviewed by the Holocaust and Human Rights Center of Maine in 1987.

That organization had been called into being in 1985 by Gerda Haas, another Theresienstadt survivor who was a librarian at Bates College, where I shared a job teaching European history with Elizabeth Tobin. Within two years, the group of survivors and educators, Jews and Christians, was capable of initiating a project to interview survivors and liberators in Maine. Gerda's vision and leadership led us to recapture knowledge about the Holocaust that might otherwise have gone unrecorded. Gerda was among the first to be interviewed, and she conducted the interview with Sonja.

This group of eager amateurs needed help in thinking about how to conduct Holocaust interviews. Dori Laub came to Maine from New Haven to educate us in a field of study he had helped to found, videotaping survivor interviews. He was born in Czernowitz in 1937, as my grandfather was a generation before; Laub and his mother survived deportation to Transnistria, but his father did not. As a psychiatrist in New Haven, he began videotaping survivors in 1979, and started to offer advice to others across the country who wished to preserve these testimonies.

Thirty interviews, recorded between 1987 and 1997, are now housed in the library of the University of Maine at Augusta, open to public use. Many of them are mentioned here.

At the same time that HHRC volunteers were interviewing survivors in Maine, I began a project to locate and interview Jewish refugees from Nazi Germany who had escaped to Shanghai. Inspired by my first interview with my grandmother, I talked with 100 former Shanghai Jews, and learned the value of oral history. I also began to teach the Holocaust in 1992. Theodore Zev Weiss, who had just founded the Holocaust Educational Foundation in Chicago, used his considerable powers of persuasion to encourage me to develop a Holocaust history course at Bates College. Many forces from outside and within inspired me to become a Holocaust teacher and scholar.

Many people believe that the best way to gain knowledge about the Holocaust is to hear from an eyewitness. The possibilities for us to do that are sadly disappearing. Educators in museums, in schools and universities, and in the media have seized on interviews as a powerful alternative. The live voices can outlive their owners.

My involvement in these two interview projects led me to attempt to transform voices into print. Producing a printed transcript was the first step. Cyrille White created draft transcriptions of most of the HHRC interviews. I was able to finish, print, and bind the interviews used here, with the help of some Bates students, Kate Caivano, Megan Goggins, and Sarah Rigney, and a consummate professional transcriber, Nicci Leamon.

Reading other people's conversations is rarely interesting and often confusing. My hope to produce a book which could allow Kurt and Sonja to teach us about the Holocaust, now and in the future, led me back to them in 2004. They once again sat down in front of a recorder to tell us more. I have edited Kurt's and Sonja's interviews to allow them to tell the stories they chose, as they happened, in their own words.

Authors produce text, but not yet books. To reshape text into a book, Robert Bernheim, who became executive director of the HHRC in 2007, offered to act as publisher. He located photographs with the help of Kurt and Sonja's children, Michael Messerschmidt and Eva Polisner. He organized fundraising to cover the cost of producing an earlier version of this book. Shenna Bellows, current HHRC director, continued the encouragement and the financial support. Erica Nadelhalf of HHRC made insightful suggestions on the guides for students and teachers. Danny Spungen of the Florence and Laurence Spungen Family Foundation offered crucial financial support for publication. Sarah Cushman of the Holocaust Educational Foundation wrote the Preface and improved the manuscript with thoughtful comments.

The final step has been taken by Alessandra Anzani and the professionals at Academic Studies Press in Boston. Without a professional publisher, books cannot find their intended audience.

This very disparate team was brought together by a belief in the power and necessity of Holocaust storytelling.

Preface

SARAH M. CUSHMAN

Director of The Holocaust Educational Foundation
of Northwestern University

"Learning remains the best antidote to humanity's most inhumane impulses." These words of Theodore Zev Weiss, the founder of the Holocaust Educational Foundation, ring as true today in 2021 as they did nearly 20 years ago when first uttered. Advancing teaching and learning about the Holocaust at the university level remains central to the mission of the Foundation (now at Northwestern University), where today I am proud to be director.

Weiss established the Holocaust Educational Foundation in 1976, with learning about the Holocaust—one of humankind's most inhumane eras—as a means of reducing antisemitism and the potential for future genocides. Steve Hochstadt was among the early professors whom Weiss contacted and encouraged to teach about the Holocaust. Then at Bates College in Maine, Hochstadt took up the call. In addition to introducing this topic to a broad array of students and involving them in recording oral histories of Holocaust survivors in Maine, Hochstadt also learned of the story of Kurt and Sonja Messerschmidt. The book that Hochstadt offers here, a project long in the making, is part of the antidote Weiss identified. It offers a view into the horrific past that is accessible to high school and college students alike. Weaving a concise history of the Holocaust with the intertwined stories of Kurt and Sonja Messerschmidt, Hochstadt creates an important introduction to the Holocaust.

In Holocaust education around the United States, best practices have established that scholarship, a grounding in the history, the facts of the event, combined with survivor testimony engages students with both the massive scale of the atrocity and its impact on individual lives. Students come to understand something of the complexity of the Holocaust, the inhumanity of hateful ideologies, and the human behavior of an array of people: perpetrators, those they targeted, those who stood by, and those who tried to intervene.

Writing this short preface brings me great satisfaction. My own work centers on the experiences of women during the Holocaust. Kurt and Sonja's stories bring to light some of the gendered aspects of the Holocaust. In addition, I went to college and lived in Maine for about a decade. I am encouraged to know that this book will be available to students across the state. Offering a local connection brings the events of the Holocaust closer to students' lives and experiences, engaging them even more deeply with this history. Students throughout the country also will benefit from the history and stories presented here.

With *Death and Love*, Hochstadt's labor of love brings Holocaust history to college and high school students and honors the individual histories of Kurt and Sonja Messerschmidt.

Introduction

Every Holocaust story is unique. Six million Jewish lives ended in six million different deaths. Even when hundreds of Jews were killed at once in a gas chamber, or tens of thousands were shot together in killing fields like Babi Yar, each life story was singular, unrepeatable and worth retelling.

Those stories were all shortened by untimely death. Except for a few diarists, we will never know much about their Holocaust experiences. We have come to rely on the Holocaust stories of a much smaller group, those who survived the camps and ghettos or who lived in hiding, to allow us glimpses into that unimaginable world. Looking back on their improbable journeys to liberation, many survivors say they persevered so they could tell the world what happened to them and to those who did not survive.

Survivors from the same town, of the same camp, even in the same family, tell different stories. Although external conditions might have been similar, what each person saw, thought, and can tell us was shaped by personality and chance, then and now. We learn something important from the hundredth description of a Nazi roundup, of a day in the Warsaw ghetto, or of a barracks in Auschwitz. There can never be enough testimonies to satisfy our need to know about how the Holocaust happened.

The stories of Sonja and Kurt Messerschmidt are singular even beyond the uniqueness of each survivor. They were among the last Jews deported from Berlin. Only a handful of couples were married in Theresienstadt, and Kurt and Sonja are possibly the only pair who survived to describe their wedding. Kurt was one of two survivors of a group of death marchers in southern Germany. Their stories are as improbable as they are moving.

The structure of this book is also unusual. In recent years, a few books have presented interviews with survivors, usually edited to make the original conversations more readable. Here two separate but always intertwined stories are juxtaposed to tell from both sides how a loving relationship formed in persecution became an element of survival in the Holocaust.

Because the experiences of Holocaust survivors are unimaginable for the rest of us, their choices of words are crucial to their ability to communicate across this gulf in understanding. My many conversations with survivors have taught me the humbling lesson that I can best express their history by letting them speak. I want to bring the curiosity, empathy, astonishment, and friendship of our conversations to the world. Conversation is like life, not a smooth narrative, but a spontaneous creation. The language of interviews is immediate, emotional, and unpolished. Because we see our listeners, we can be more revealing. Conversation about the past brings forth the passion that is often harder to perceive in written narratives. Although the conversational moment is now past, something of the emotion and intimacy of the interviews remains in these printed words.

Kurt and Sonja were interviewed as part of the project by the HHRC to record and preserve individual experiences of Holocaust survivors. Those raw interviews, and the thousands of survivor interviews done across the world since 1945, form the building blocks from which the evolving history of the Holocaust must be written.

I believe these interviews with the Messerschmidts can be even more than building blocks. Because they begin with the Nazi seizure of power in 1933, step through all of the stages of the developing genocide, and bring us into the present, Kurt and Sonja can introduce the reader to the vast scope of the most horrifying and significant event of the twentieth century.

To accomplish that, my work also appears on every page. All the words quoted in these chapters were spoken by the narrators. But these stories are not reproduced here exactly as they were told. Transcripts of interviews are difficult to read. As in any conversation, we change direction in the middle of sentences, interrupt, correct or repeat ourselves. Not everything said is equally relevant to the main story. I have selected a third to a half of the content of the interviews. I have reordered anecdotes and sentences to shape a chronological narrative—the order of telling has become the same as the order of happening. The voices remain those of Sonja and Kurt.

Why is this still important in the twenty-first century? During my years of teaching the Holocaust to audiences across the world, I have learned that hearing a Holocaust story obligates the listener to do something. Holocaust stories force us to think again about life, our lives, our society's life, humanity itself. Kurt and Sonja have much more to tell us than their own lives.

Berlin

When the National Socialist German Workers Party (NSDAP) was born in a meeting room in Munich in 1919, their dreams of a German future excluded Jews. After Adolf Hitler pushed his way into the leadership in 1921, he introduced a vitriolic and irrational hatred for all Jews into Nazi doctrine. Like many Germans of all classes and occupations at that time, he was open about hating Jews, but he also harbored a deep desire to get rid of them entirely that few Germans shared. His political speeches during the 1920s, as the Nazis gradually won recognition among Germans, and especially his memoir and manifesto, *Mein Kampf*, published in 1925, displayed Hitler's extremism on "the Jewish question" for everyone to see. Whatever he was thinking when he wrote "All who are not of good race in this world are chaff," his language went far beyond what the leaders of less radical political parties said.[1]

What Hitler meant was demonstrated by the violence of his supporters against people they considered "chaff." One thousand men of the armed and uniformed Nazi *Sturmabteilung*, usually called the SA, attacked Jews all over Berlin on the Jewish New Year in September 1931. They unleashed a terror campaign in eastern Germany just before the elections of 1932, killing hundreds of leftists, Poles, and Jews in bombings, shootings, and arson. In that election, the Nazis won 37% and became the largest party in the Reichstag, the German parliament, where no party or faction had a majority. German conservatives thought they could use Hitler and the Nazis to retain power, so President Paul von Hindenburg appointed him Chancellor on January 30, 1933.

About 525,000 Jews lived in Germany when Hitler became Chancellor and the Nazis began to transform Germany into the Thousand-Year Reich. Jews made up about 1% of the German population, but the Nazis asserted that Jews were a foreign race of subhuman beings, exerting extraordinary powers over "real Germans." Jews had been responsible for Germany's loss in World War I,

---

1   Adolf Hitler, *Mein Kampf*, translated by Ralph Manheim (Boston: Houghton Mifflin, 1971), p. 296.

for the Depression and high unemployment that had brought the Nazis to power, and for defiling the blood of innocent German women and girls. At last someone was going to take action against this deadly threat to the future of the Aryan race.

Yet when the Nazis started to dismantle the Weimar democratic system that had been so contentious since its creation in 1919, their initial targets were not Jews. After the Reichstag building, the German parliament, was set on fire on February 28, 1933, Hitler blamed Communists and suspended constitutional civil liberties. Under pressure, the Reichstag passed the Enabling Act in March, giving Hitler virtually dictatorial powers. Dachau, the first concentration camp, was hastily created and immediately filled with thousands of Communists and other political opponents. Freely employing deadly and public violence, brown-shirted Stormtroopers and black-shirted SS troops grabbed labor leaders, leftist and liberal political leaders, and writers, and threw them into makeshift jails. Ninety-six members of the Reichstag were eventually murdered by the Nazis.

Once they had consolidated unchallenged political power by transforming German democracy into a Nazi dictatorship, Hitler and his inner circle began to put into practice their antisemitic racism. The Nazis tried to separate Jews from German society and economy. On April 1, the Nazi government began a public boycott of all Jewish businesses, calling on all patriotic Germans to eliminate Jewish influence on the national economy. Despite stationing uniformed Stormtroopers in front of Jewish stores and offices, the boycott was a failure. Nazi ambitions were far in advance of ordinary Germans, who refused to change their daily shopping habits so quickly.

Over the next five years, the Nazis gradually attacked Jews by decree. The Nuremberg Laws of September 1935 eliminated Jews' rights as citizens and identified them as barely tolerated aliens. Bank accounts and automobiles were confiscated, businesses were closed or taken over, organizations were made illegal, Jewish students were thrown out of public schools and prevented from getting university degrees. Jews lost their jobs as judges, railroad workers, doctors in public hospitals, army officers, university professors and schoolteachers. By 1938, over 60% of all businesses that had been owned by Jews before the Nazis took power had disappeared.[2]

---

2   Marion A. Kaplan, *Between Dignity and Despair: Jewish Life in Nazi Germany* (New York: Oxford University Press, 1998), p. 28.

At the same time, the Nazis attacked other groups they identified as biologically and morally inferior: homosexual men, who threatened the rapid propagation of the Aryan race; Roma and Sinti, whose working and living habits did not match Nazi standards; the mentally and physically disabled, who cost the nation valuable resources; and Jehovah's Witnesses, who refused to acknowledge the authority of the Nazi state. New concentration camps, such as Sachsenhausen near Berlin and Buchenwald outside of Weimar, were added to hold the endless list of enemies behind barbed wire, where they could be humiliated, beaten, and killed out of public sight.

Except for those who happened to fall into one of these despised categories, or who pursued romantic relationships with non-Jewish partners, German Jews were not usually physically attacked in the first years of Nazi power. That may be one reason why most Jews tried to survive in Germany. Between 1933 and 1937, about 130,000 left the country, 25% of the total. A more decisive reason why more did not leave was the difficulty of finding a country that would accept them. Although United States law allowed about 27,000 Germans to enter the country every year, bureaucratic obstacles were created to prevent any more than 20% of that number from entering the US. Great Britain, France, Switzerland, and other desirable destinations for German Jews desperate to flee the expanding persecution at home made immigration more and more difficult, targeting especially Jews. That is why the Swiss government suggested to the Nazis that a prominent "J" be stamped into the passports of German Jews, so that the border guards could selectively turn Jews away.

In 1938, Nazi political leaders and ordinary citizens turned to more public and violent tactics. After Austrians greeted their incorporation into Greater Germany in March 1938 with joyous parades and adulation for Hitler himself, they turned on the Jews in their midst with hatred and greed. Scenes of jeering adults surrounding Jewish women and men on their knees, scrubbing paint off the cobblestones, represent the racist anger that erupted in Vienna, a city of about 180,000 Jews. Mobs sprinkled with Stormtroopers danced in the streets shouting, "Perish the Jews!"[3] In the first week, the extreme violence prompted Reinhard Heydrich to threaten to arrest Party members who "allowed themselves to launch large-scale assaults in a totally undisciplined way." During the rest of March, 79 Viennese Jews committed suicide; the violence only died

---

3   The *Daily Telegraph*'s Vienna correspondent, G. E. R. Gedye, wrote about what he saw during those days in *Fallen Bastions: The Central European Tragedy* (London: 1939).

down in April. A few weeks later half of all Jewish businesses in Vienna had been seized, including 78 of 86 Jewish-owned banks.[4]

The violence and pace of government attacks on Jews across Germany now increased. On June 9, the synagogue in Munich was destroyed by a mob led by Nazi officials. A week later, 1,500 Jews who had prior legal problems, including traffic tickets, were arrested and sent to Buchenwald. Violence against Jews was always accompanied by plunder. Most Jews who still had jobs or businesses now lost them. New concentration camps were established, like Neuengamme near Hamburg and Mauthausen in Austria.

In October 1938, 16,000 Jews with Polish citizenship were put into cattle cars and dumped over the Polish border. When a young Polish Jew named Herschel Grynszpan, whose parents had just been forcibly deported, shot and killed a German diplomat in Paris on November 7, Hitler and his propaganda minister Josef Goebbels seized this pretext to attack all Jews with force. On the night of November 9, since then usually called *Kristallnacht*, Jewish businesses, synagogues, and apartments were destroyed across the Third Reich, and dozens of Jews brutally murdered. Thirty thousand Jewish men were arrested and put into Dachau, Buchenwald and Sachsenhausen concentration camps. Blaming the Jews for the attacks on them, Reich Minister Hermann Göring fined the German Jewish community 1 billion Marks (around $7.5 billion in today's US dollars), vastly accelerating the plunder of Jewish property.

The isolation of Jews from German society and the plunder of their possessions continued into 1939. Jewish children were thrown out of public schools and forced to attend all-Jewish schools. Jews had to surrender all their gold and silver. In a speech to the Reichstag on January 30, 1939, six years after taking power, Hitler threatened that if war broke out in Europe, Jews would face extermination.

German and Austrian Jews suddenly realized that their very survival was threatened. The stream of refugees out of the Third Reich became a flood in 1938 and 1939. The Western democracies selectively relaxed some of their restrictions on immigration: Great Britain allowed 10,000 Jewish children to enter through the so-called *Kindertransport*, but without their parents; the bureaucratic hurdles to getting visas into the US were lowered so that more Jewish immigrants could enter in 1939. Much less desirable destinations became treasured refuges for desperate Jews: 16,000 German-speaking Jews

4 Saul Friedländer, *Nazi Germany and the Jews, v. 1, The Years of Persecution, 1933–1939* (New York: HarperCollins, 1997), pp. 242–243.

fled to Shanghai in 1938 and 1939, and perhaps as many as 20,000 to Bolivia, before those possibilities were also closed off.

But only a minority of the Jews left in the Third Reich were able to get out of Europe. The 938 passengers of the SS *St. Louis*, refused entry to Cuba and then to the US, symbolized the plight of all those who desperately wanted to flee.

Although he constantly asserted that Jews would be responsible for any war, Hitler himself now sent his armies across the German borders. In March 1939, German troops occupied Czechoslovakia. After concluding a secret agreement with the Soviet Union to divide Poland, the Nazis invaded Poland on September 1, crushing all resistance in four weeks. Finally the British and French reacted and World War II officially began.

So also began the Holocaust. War provided the Nazi leadership with the distraction they needed to begin mass killings of racially inferior peoples. In Poland special troops named *Einsatzgruppen* began rounding up Jews and shooting them. Over 16,000 Polish civilians, Jews and Catholics, were killed in the first six weeks after the invasion.

At the same time, mentally and physically disabled Germans were murdered under the so-called T4 program organized by Hitler's direct subordinates and German doctors. After experimenting with deadly injections and starvation, poison gas as a method of mass murder was first tried out on 20 disabled patients in January 1940 in an asylum near Berlin. Eventually 70,000 disabled Germans and many more Poles were killed under the auspices of T4.

There were far too many Jews in Poland, over 3 million, to kill them all by shooting. Ghettos were immediately created by the Nazis in larger Polish cities and Jews from all over the country were herded into Warsaw, Łódź, and a few other central locations, as a first step towards the still unspecified "final solution."

The war made it nearly impossible for German Jews to leave the country, so the Nazi government shifted its focus from encouraging emigration to organizing deportation. In February 1940 the first deportations from Germany to "the East" began. Mass shootings of Polish Jews increased. The lightning defeat of Holland, Belgium, and France in May 1940 brought another half million Jews under Nazi control, as German armies began to appear invincible.

In June 1941, Hitler took the next logical step in his plan to conquer all of Europe: his armies suddenly invaded the Soviet Union. As German tanks and troops pushed hundreds of miles into Soviet territory, the *Einsatzgruppen* unleashed genocidal violence on the Jews of eastern Europe. In two days in

September 1941, over 33,000 Jews from Kiev were shot at Babi Yar. Although it is impossible to be precise, at least 1.5 million Jews were taken out of their homes, sometimes forced to dig their own graves, and shot by SS troops, regular soldiers, and specially recruited police battalions on the Eastern Front, from Latvia to Yugoslavia. Even more millions of Soviet civilians died at the hands of the Germans.

Back at home, the Jews of Berlin were forced into slave labor for the German military. But their days were numbered. On January 20, 1942, representatives of various government ministries met at a villa in the Berlin suburb of Wannsee, presided over by Reinhard Heydrich, Heinrich Himmler's number two man in the SS. Plans for the murder of all the Jews of Europe were calmly developed. By then the Holocaust was in full swing.

Sonja and Kurt spent these years in the Nazi capital, Berlin, staging ground for killings elsewhere.

Sonja Messerschmidt: My name is Sonja Messerschmidt and my maiden name was Kolbelsky. My father's family came from Finland and Poland. My parents were born both in Berlin. They married and lived in Berlin and had all their children in Berlin.[5] I only mention that because none of us were ever German citizens. We had to apply for citizenship, and they never did.

I was born in Berlin in 1925, and I was an only child. That is where I grew up and went to school, and that's where I lived until I was arrested and deported.

We were anything but rich. My father was a traveling salesman, but I don't think he was a very good businessman, because we just got by all the time. I had friends who came from really well-to-do families and had a lot of things I never had, but I keep saying that children don't mind. I never thought of myself as poor. I always felt wonderful for what other kids had, and they would let me use some of their toys, and in that respect I had a happy childhood.

Kurt Messerschmidt: Well, my story is completely different. I'm much older, so my story starts at the beginning of World War I, and my youth

---

5 Sonja's father Sally Kolbelsky was born in Berlin in 1896. Her mother Emmy Sonn is listed as having been born in Smoldzino, Poland, in 1897. There were married in Berlin in 1921.

fell into the post-World War I years of the inflation, which impoverished my mother and grandparents.[6] Father had passed on long ago, and we were totally impoverished when we came and moved into Berlin in 1918. I was three years old. My mother was twice divorced. My brother lived with my mother throughout the entire time. I for some reason developed talents, and nobody had ever suspected, I was kind of, not a genius, but way above average in many respects.

Berlin was a fantastic city. There were so many possibilities, which I haven't found in any other place. I went to the public school for the first four years and was so fantastic a student, I don't believe it myself now, that they forced me into the *Gymnasium*, the highest school where nobody was easily accepted. My mother, I remember, was standing in front of the gate waiting for the results of the test, and I see myself coming out and speaking to her, "Go home, Mom, it's a piece of cake." And so she was satisfied with that.

But being satisfied with that was not enough. Of course, she had not the means to be of any support for the things I would need to really make this education a piece of reality. I could list about ten wonderful people, who knew about me at the time and set everything into motion to make it possible for me to get the highest possible education. And they insisted and convinced my mother that it had to be done. It was a very hard decision for her to let me go, but she had one son at home. It was the finest boarding school you can imagine. That education gave me my Jewish upbringing, but not just Orthodox. I was exposed to Orthodoxy, to liberal Judaism, and especially the music appealed to me a great deal. And my other education, the one that was the supposed to become my profession, was the *humanistisches Gymnasium*, the humanistic education which stressed languages, especially the classics, and all the fine arts. But this was the non-Jewish school, the *Lessing Gymnasium* in Berlin, later the *Humboldt Gymnasium*.[7] In my class they had only one more Jewish fellow, Knopf, brilliant in his teens, a philosopher in his own right. He could debate our German professors

---

6   Kurt was born in 1915.
7   The Lessing Gymnasium in Berlin was founded in 1882. It served as a preparatory school for boys until girls were admitted in 1927. Under the Nazis, girls were no longer admitted. Although the school has been moved several times, it continues as a renowned institution. The Humboldt Gymnasium in Berlin was founded in 1903, with an emphasis on Latin and French.

easily about Hegel and Marx, this was a few years before Hitler really came to power.

So I had this wonderful exposure to the general education and the Jewish education. Had two sets of friends, two sets of worlds I lived in, and happily could combine these two, which I think I benefit from to this very day. And so I was never a radical Orthodox Jew, although I could walk into any very Orthodox community and worship with them in their personal way, being quite happy seeing them happy. My main enjoyment was the music, full choirs and classical approaches to music, even to Jewish music.

So this was my upbringing. Languages were my life. At age ten, I started Latin. At age twelve, they added French, which was an easy connection. Then came the biggest step at age thirteen, Greek. Two years later, Spanish. And then, strangely enough, only during the very last two years, English, which was looked down upon as the language of merchants. I wanted to become a linguist. Only French was taught as conversational language. Of course, we had the literature, too, and I was working constantly with the big volumes, the Greek dictionaries, and translating Homer and Demosthenes. I was about eighteen years old when I was asked to work with a professor, Sigmund Feist, on a Gothic dictionary. Because of my knowledge of so many other languages, I could proofread and have my own suggestions. This was my goal until 1933 arrived.

January 30, 1933, I can never forget, the day the Nazis came to power. The night before I attended a theater performance. I remember going by streetcar to the theater in the Kommandantenstrasse. And standing in the streetcar, all of a sudden, we were stopped. There were marching masses of people carrying torches. This was the great torch march of the Nazis celebrating their taking over the power. That's when my life took a complete turnabout.

I was very active in sports, which impressed my non-Jewish classmates, who had been practicing their German *Sieg Heil* greeting for a few years already. I had won their respect.

I remember our final oral exams, especially the Latin oral exam. We were all in one room and you went in to meet the commission, with their insignia, high Nazi officials. And while we were sitting in the anteroom preparing the portions of Cicero or whatever it was, all of my classmates asked me to help them. I helped every one of them, pushed them through the door. "You go, you are ready, you do it." And then came my own. My teachers were so proud of me. My Latin professor almost embarrassed me, because he was so sure that what he asked me I would be able to do. My private home reading for this exam had been *Agricola* by Tacitus, and I had been allowed to conduct classes for him when he had to go to some other room or something. And so he asked me, "Herr Messerschmidt, you studied *Agricola*. Would you be able to recite for us? What portion impressed you most?" There was no question it was the final paragraph, which was fantastic. I did it and it was a highlight for my professor, who was so proud of the Jewish child there, the Jewish young man.

Here everything positive stops, because the next day I received a postcard in the mail. Like you have here high school proms, affairs where you celebrate your graduation, there was something they called a *Kommers*. It was for gentlemen only, a lot of drinking and all of this kind of stuff. It's a big thing in the life of a German student. And this postcard simply stated, "For our concluding celebration, Jews are not desired." Those were the ones who had been my friends until the day before. And the next day, they were not.

I did not live at home with my mother through my exams in 1933. Then we were forced together as a family again, because we had to consider emigrating as a family. So that's when we came very close space wise, very close in love and harmony and every other respect, because I loved my brother. There's nothing that can describe the love we have for each other, even though we are very far apart now.

Sonja: Though my father came from a religious background, his parents coming from the East, our home was not religious, was very assimilated, because my mother's family was very assimilated.

So we really did not observe holidays in our home. But we would go to other relatives and spend holidays with them. Or if my parents didn't, then I would. Many holidays I spent just with Jewish friends. I would seek out relatives who were observant or friends who were. And you were always welcome in somebody else's home for holidays.

I went to German schools until 1936, I believe, or '35. By then Jewish children were not allowed to attend public German schools anymore. Because of Hitler, of course, I had to be transferred and I was very happy to be transferred at that point.

I attended a Jewish parochial school, Rykestrasse it was called. When I made the switch, I was either ten or eleven. And it turned out to be just wonderful to be with all Jewish children, especially after the treatment we received during the last year or so in the public school. It wasn't so much the teachers, it was the hatred of the children, who teased us or told us that we really didn't belong, that we were only guests, so to speak. All of a sudden you didn't belong anymore. The whole thing was hard to understand for a child. My parents didn't dare explain too much to me, because they were afraid, too, of what I might say that could endanger them.

My father traveled a lot and he lost a lot of his business. Financially, even then, I could understand that we were under a great deal of trouble.

The Christian friends I had withdrew, probably because their parents told them not to play with me anymore. That's why it was such a relief to be in a school with all Jewish children. All of a sudden, you were so much part of everything, and you could have friends again, friends that would come to visit you and would ask you to come to their house. That didn't exist anymore with the other children. That's actually when I learned a lot about Jewish customs and loved them, though I did not see them at home.

I loved being there until I graduated after the eighth grade, because that was the end of it. And I became an apprentice for a very, very fine seamstress, a dressmaker, and stayed with her for about two years, until she received a phone call and she had to let me go. And from that time on I had to do forced labor. So did my parents.

There were a lot of cousins, first cousins, second cousins. At the time there were still a few brothers and sisters of my parents. But on my father's side, they left. His brother was killed, he was the first one who died in a concentration camp, and all his brothers left Germany in the thirties still.[8]

My mother's family, the only brother my mother had, he left Germany in the dark of night and he fled with his family to Belgium.

---

8   Sonja's uncle Hermann Kolbelsky was arrested in June 1938 and died in Sachsenhausen concentration camp in 1943.

But he didn't survive it either, because he was caught there.⁹ And my mother's two sisters were married to Christian men, and they both survived. Their husbands stood by them. One uncle lost his job, but both husbands stayed with their wives. Some did not survive regardless of Christian husbands, but they were fortunate.

Kurt: In '33, in April, I finished my *Gymnasium* and would have been ready to enter the university. Hitler had come to power already. My goal was a university career, teaching and research in languages. My *Direktor*, the school principal, was a fantastic person, a philosopher and educator of highest degree, of course a non-Nazi. Since I was such an outstanding student, but my family were not the richest people in the world, he proposed my name for a complete scholarship from the German Students' [Organization], *Deutsches Studentenwerk*. He showed extreme courage to do this and I will always be grateful for that. So I had the interview with the high Nazi official, with his swastika symbol. Of course, nothing could come of it.

I applied in '33 to get into Berlin University into my field. It was already impossible for me as Jew. I was able to get into the Berlin University through the so-called Oriental Seminary, where they taught languages, Oriental languages, African dialects, any kind of language. At the time I was considering, with the help of friends, to move to a big firm in the Far East near the Mongolian border. I could have been employed as an interpreter for that particular firm. Latin and Greek was not required, but French, Spanish, English, and other languages I knew quite well up to that point, that was a given. But I needed in addition Chinese and Russian, so I entered this Oriental Seminary in Berlin University for one year.

But then I was discouraged because the cultural situation of the Far East, the things we have here every day now, drugs, sex, all the impossible things. For me, who grew up studying the classics and was always up there in the higher sphere, was impossible even to consider. I gave that idea up.

Other things were happening. At that point the Nazis started planning what developed later into some kind of a ghettoization.

---

9   Sonja's uncle Siegfried Sonn was put into a concentration camp in France, then deported to Auschwitz, where he was killed. His son Meinhard Sonn was also killed in Auschwitz.

Within Berlin the government circle, the Wilhelmstrasse, was off-limits for Jews. It went further, into the school system, and Jewish children, like my wife, who at the time still attended non-Jewish schools, had to leave. For this they needed schools suddenly. But there were not enough schools for all these children.

So the Jewish community, encouraged, in quotation marks, by the Nazis, had to think of training people who would work as teachers and cantors in schools to be established all over the country. With the encouragement of the Nazis, there was a teachers' academy formed to train Jewish teachers and cantors to teach these new to-be-created Jewish schools. I immediately qualified, because for this teachers' seminar and cantors' institute my background was way above what was required. I had known Hebrew also for many years. So I enrolled there. It was a three-year course, but I was overqualified, so it was abbreviated for me to two years, because of my previous background.

Then I applied to the existing schools. There was a Goldschmidt School, it was a wonderful school. They had plenty of means and could offer their students the best possible. You would have very small classes, so ideal set ups. I auditioned there and gave lessons, and it was very interesting, small classes and brilliant kids. But they didn't have the need for me as somebody who could be more than just a teacher. For them that was a transit situation, emigration would be essential, teach me and we'll leave. It wouldn't enter into any personal warm relationship between the students and their families.

This is what the *Rykeschule* in the Rykestrasse offered. This was a very special school. The school director was Frau Schiratzki, an extremely unusual person, an educator, small size, a giant in every other respect. It also had coeducation program, boys and girls together.[10] The other Jewish schools, boys' schools, they all wanted me, I auditioned

---

10 Selma Schiratzki was born in Frankfurt in 1890. The co-educational Jewish school in Rykestrasse was founded in the 1920s, and Schiratzki became headmistress in 1926. It became a place of refuge for Jewish students thrown out of German public schools. The day after *Kristallnacht*, a mob of adults and children attacked the empty school, smashed windows, and destroyed books and musical instruments. In 1941, the German Army confiscated the school and turned it into a military post office. After the war, Schiratzki moved to Israel, where she died in 1980. She wrote about the school: "The Rykestrasse School in Berlin: A Jewish Elementary School during the Hitler Period," Leo Baeck Institute Yearbook (1960), 5(1): 299–307.

everywhere, everybody wanted me. But I insisted on this particular school and I never regretted it. I felt they needed me, and I needed them. I got to know the family backgrounds, and many spoke at home still Polish or Yiddish, but I had to teach the real German literature. I taught every subject imaginable. In addition, of course, we taught Hebrew as a language and prayer language.

That's where Sonja entered the picture. My wife at the time was a student at that school, and she was about to be graduated shortly after I had started.

Sonja: I was his student. And actually you started as a student teacher.

I heard that Kurt Messerschmidt had become our prime teacher, and I was very upset. "My God," I said, "He's so skinny." [laughs] How old was I? I think twelve? At the most. [laughs] He became our teacher, and that's really how we met. And actually not 'till I left school did we become, there was a whole group of us who were, we still stayed friendly with our teacher. And, of course he was pretty close to our age compared to other teachers, and you even were invited to our house, you came to visit. And this is how really slowly a romance began. I'm sure my parents weren't happy about it, and your mother wasn't crazy about me, because there was an age difference. But it stuck. We just celebrated our sixtieth wedding anniversary, so whoever said it wouldn't last?

Kurt: All of a sudden there was this lovely person there. You see, you get to know people if you have to give them topics to write, compositions, and you see the handwritings and you can exactly enter their minds. And there was a wonderful mind, it was fantastic what Sonja did, it was such a maturity that floored me. And she was not the only one. This was a whole group of children, well, there were no children, with the outer pressures they had to face at home and outside of the home.

This was a, well, the proof of the pudding is some of them did survive, over sixty years ago, they did survive and found my name via the Internet somewhere. One of them lived in Basel, he was able to emigrate, he had I think Romanian citizenship, so he could emigrate any time he wanted to, and he ended up finally in Switzerland, lived in Basel. He was the first one to find my name. And he contacted a number of his former classmates who also were able to emigrate, some under very difficult circumstances, but they didn't have to go to any concentration camps. They went to Shanghai, for instance, and so there was all of a sudden, of this group, somebody in Basel, in Berlin, in London, in Israel, and some in the States. He got them all together, and we had a reunion, in London the first time. Of the whole group we were the only ones who had survived concentration camps, which means apparently that many of the others, if they didn't happen to emigrate somehow, would not have survived. So it was a very bittersweet reunion, but it was something.

We had to prepare our children for emigration. The number one point was Israel and England and America and South America, so I taught Hebrew, English, Spanish, in addition to practically every other subject.

Emigration was on my mind. Preparing my students and their families for emigration, of course it had to enter my mind, too. You know, the need to be needed is the most satisfying thing there can be. I think I was never needed as much as in those years when I taught in that school. Shortly after I had started, the factories were filled with the parents of those children I was teaching. The children were left to themselves and I had to be more than just teacher. I had to be friend, I had to be father and mother, protector, everything in one person. I was the home away from home for those students whose parents were sweating already in Hitler's factories.

This Frau Schiratzki, she gave me complete freedom, in America the administration would never allow this, so I was teaching history and literature, I could combine this. I would talk about the French Revolution, Napoleon, and I used Emil Ludwig as a literary example also.[11] I had them read out loud. These were wonderful things. When I gave them any homework assignments and I had to correct those, and when some of those kids read something out loud, I was amazed at the maturity of these young people, in spite or because of all the pressures they were under. And so that of course brought us somehow together.

Sonja was in one of my Spanish courses also in school, while it still was operating. And she was in the choir, too, terrific. Oh, the orchestra, she played the mandolin. I discovered that talent.

---

11 Emil Ludwig (1881–1948) was a prolific German-Swiss author, who wrote biographies of Napoleon, Bismarck, and Lincoln.

After school we still met, the class came back and back, we had all kinds of meetings. We played ping-pong and chess and everything, it was something that extended way beyond any classroom activity.

That brings me to 1938, November 9, the so-called Crystal Night. In the morning of November 10, 1938, at the same time, most of the synagogues all over Germany were set to flame.

My transportation in those days was bicycle. I had to ride about seven miles to get to the school where I was teaching. And that morning, I rode this bicycle through the city of Berlin and all I could see was broken glass. All the stores, large and small, were completely ruined. I got to my school, to my classroom, some of the children had arrived and were sitting in their seats in tears. So all I could do is try to calm them down a little bit. It was an unbelievable situation. Our own conference room had been ravaged. I had in a big closet about ten musical instruments, which I had given to the children and taught them every instrument we had. All this was stolen.

And one thing I remember especially. If you are a very Orthodox Jew and a very liberal Jew, there are things where they just cannot get together. One of my students, Esther Zeitman, came in a little late and she broke down in tears. She had seen the great liberal synagogue in flames. It touched me that this very Orthodox child could be touched by a liberal synagogue being harmed. But we were all one.

We had been relocated in the Chorinerstrasse. Across from our school there was a memorial of one of the martyrs of the early Nazi days, the twenties. So there was a guard standing in front of our school. And at the corner there was a large group of non-Jewish children armed with rocks just waiting for the children to come out. The children had to get out. They had to try to somehow get home. So I felt like Moses of old, leading the children of Israel through the Red Sea. I stood up to my full height, looking directly at those children, and somehow I believe I was convincing at that particular moment. They did not throw a stone. They let our children go by.

After that, a dear colleague of mine who did not survive Auschwitz, Rudi Sonnenfeld, a sports coach, and I took our bicycles and toured the whole city.[12] I saw the synagogues burn. In the Friedrichstrasse there

---

12 Rudi Sonnenfeld was born about 1908. He taught at the Rykestrasse school and was coach of a Jewish girls' gymnastics club in Berlin. He was murdered in Auschwitz in 1943.

was one small tobacco store, and the owner was a very old Jewish gentleman. The SA, the ones in the brown shirts, were standing there forcing this man, who could hardly stand, to pick up the glass pieces. The people were all standing around saying nothing. Nobody moved. So the two of us put our bikes down and went to pick up the glass for this man. We full well knew what could have happened. In those days, it would have been easy for them to arrest us and send us off. But nobody dared say anything. Some of the people standing there very silently and very cautiously agreed to what we were doing.

Then I came to what used to be my school before we were relocated, the synagogue in the Rykestrasse. Saw the flames coming up. The firemen were there with their hoses. I realized soon what they were doing. The synagogue was in the back yard. They had to protect the adjoining buildings from the fire, to make sure the job was well done.[13]

At that point, I think my will to live and to outlive everybody became so strong that I think it helped me later on.

Sonja: Before the outbreak of the war there was still a possibility for children to leave in transports. A cousin of mine did go. I was assigned to a transport to go to England. I refused. I was an only child and I just couldn't tear myself away.[14]

I was an apprentice for a very fine seamstress, I and another Jewish girl, and she received a phone call to let us go. We had to report to the unemployment office. There we were told that from the next day on, we would be working for the factory, for a Siemens cable company. We spun fiberglass that they used to cover cables. It definitely was a war effort. It was forced labor.

My mother, who did not work at all, also was forced into forced labor for the same company, Siemens. They had many factories all over the city, and though we worked for the same company, we were in different places. My father lost even the little business that he had, because he was not German, they declared him stateless. He had to

---

13 Because the Rykestrasse synagogue was located inside a block of residential buildings, it was not destroyed, as were most synagogues in the Third Reich. Instead, the Nazis burned Torah scrolls, smashed furniture, and then put out the fire.

14 Great Britain admitted about 10,000 children from Germany, Austria, and Czechoslovakia without their parents in 1938 and 1939 in the so-called *Kindertransport* (children's transports). Most of the parents did not survive.

work for the railroad, he did railroad tracks, and it was very heavy work. But he was an optimist, so he could joke about it. They gave him rubber boots for bad weather, and he said they were absolutely waterproof, because once the water got in there, it never got out. As things got worse and worse, my mother suggested that we all turn on the gas and kill ourselves, that we go together. But my father wouldn't hear of it. He said, "I have to see the end of this, how we'll all be at the end." Of course, we know how it ended. They were taken that one day, and I never saw them again.

We worked in shifts, like factories do. We came from different parts of the city and we had to meet in front of the factory, and then we were led into these big rooms where the machines were. That's where we spent our eight or nine hours, I don't remember exactly. Even to go to the bathroom, you had to have permission from the foreman, who of course was a German.

We worked in separate departments under separate supervision. We weren't free to come and go as we pleased. We were brought in in groups, we left in groups. It's just that we still lived at home, we still had our own home. As long as we had that work, we were protected. And at least we could go home to our own apartment. I actually stayed until 1943.

We became officially engaged in 1941. There were a lot of people, a lot of transports going already.[15] So we knew that we would be separated and we tried to get married. We had the idea that way we can stay together. We had no idea you don't stay together anyway. Kurt was a German citizen, I was not. I, like my father, was stateless. So we did not get permission to marry by the German government.

Kurt: My emigration plans had been shattered earlier. I had an affidavit to America, but the quota for German Jews was very small. When I finally approached the time where I could be called up, my affidavit was not sufficient. So I had to write for another one. But by then the war had broken out, it was too late.

---

15   On October 18, 1941, 1089 Jews were deported from Berlin to the Łódź ghetto, the first of many transports carrying over 50,000 Jews out of Berlin. Nearly all were murdered in the death camps.

I kept teaching in that school while the transports were going on. My classes, the numbers of children began to shrink. In June 1942, the whole Jewish school system, the system the Nazis had helped create, was closed down, because now it was time to start with the Final Solution. The moment this happened, I knew my number was up, I was ready to be transported. Because I had a job with the Jewish community as a cantor and teacher, I was protected as long as possible. Now this was gone.

I was called up to the Jewish school administration. It was a lawyer, Rechtsanwalt Schaefer, I remember him like today. He called me in and spoke to me. "Herr Messerschmidt, you know our work here is finished and you know what it means for you. We have to submit your name also now for deportation." I said, "Yes, I'm fully aware of it." "But I have a proposition for you. You are well known in our city as a teacher, a cantor. You are beloved by your students. We want to try somehow, even illegally, to continue this teaching process. We have to think of ways to do this. We found a front, and we want you to be included in this plan."

Jewish apartments, after the inhabitants had been deported, were sealed. Nobody could enter until the Gestapo came later. Then the furniture was removed and stored in various places. They needed people to do this. I was young, I was strong, I was athletic. So they thought of me, under the condition that I would try to teach underground. This sounded absolutely marvelous, because teaching and helping these youth was my life, unless I could emigrate.

I kept teaching what I had been doing before. Now I concentrated not on the music, there was no need for this, but the languages. I did this to help prepare some people, Spanish, I went from home to home, couldn't meet more than three or four people at a time, it was all forbidden.

So I continued teaching and doing the good work as long as I could. They had asked a total of ten men to do this job. It was officially for the Gestapo. We were called the *Stern* Column, had to wear the Jewish star on our work clothes. This went for one year.

So I taught this and then I schlepped the furniture for the, this I don't have to tell you, and of course I couldn't continue this much longer. But even under all this pressure, we stayed close together. And it was a *forza del destino*,[16] because the fact that I was able to work in

---

16 Kurt makes a reference here to the Verdi opera "La Forza del Destino" (The Power of Fate).

that firm, quasi for the Gestapo, that helped Sonja survive eventually. This was also an unbelievable moment.

In '43 came the big factory action, they called it *Fabrikaktion*, when all the Jews were picked up from their place of work.[17] I was caught also, although I should have been protected by the special papers I was given by the firm that did this job. So I was arrested and all of a sudden I was cut off from the world. I was the one who could support the remainders of my family. There was only my brother. My fiancée, whose parents had been deported at the end of February in '43, was all of a sudden all alone. She was fortunate not to have been at home when they came to her apartment, so she came to our apartment and stayed there.

Sonja: My family had been taken from their place of work in February 1943. They went to work in the morning and never came home.

I had been warned the night before by Kurt. All he knew was that there was something, a big action was planned for the following day. He didn't know what it would be exactly. I came home around midnight from work, and I left a note for my father to be very, very careful the following day. He was a smoker, and Jews were not allowed to buy cigarettes. He had some cigarettes on the black market, and I wanted him not to have anything on him, because I figured that would make things so much worse. I wanted him to go to work without his cigarettes. It didn't matter whether he would have had the cigarettes or not. They were all taken from their place of work. I had taken the day off, just played hooky. If I hadn't, I would have been among them. We were all working in different places, but that didn't matter. They were taken from all over Berlin, no matter where they worked.

I was at home. When the time came that my parents should have come home and they didn't, I got very uneasy and I finally went out into the street. And somebody said to me, somebody not German, we wore the yellow star, "Take the star off, they're taking people, they're grabbing them right and left, right off the street." I realized that my parents probably wouldn't come back, and I expected to be picked up

---

17 During the *Fabrikaktion* in February 1943, the Gestapo tried to round up the remaining 11,000 Jews who had been working in armaments factories in Berlin for deportation. Nearly 5,000 went into hiding, perhaps 1,500 of whom survived the war.

myself. So I went back into the apartment and I tried to prepare some food and pack it, just little bundles, anything I could carry for myself and my parents, thinking I would be picked up and taken to wherever they were. Nothing happened.

Then suddenly, my brother-in-law, who at that time was not [yet] my brother-in-law, appeared at the door. I was so happy to see him, just somebody I knew and could talk to. My brother-in-law was a carpenter at the time, his boss realized what was going on and sent him home. He did not want him to be arrested. He was a German. He told him, "Just get out of here and hide somewhere." Well, he came to me and told me that his mother had been arrested and that also his brother, Kurt, had been taken. That came as even a bigger shock to us. He was under protection, because he worked for a man who worked with the Gestapo, a mover who removed the furniture of people who had been deported and cleared out the apartments. That was a job that really gave some protection, so that when we heard that Kurt had also been arrested, we didn't know what to think of it. He was let go, by the way, after a day or maybe a few hours, I don't recall. But from that time on, the three of us were together again.

I left my apartment and moved in with Kurt and Heinz, because I was just so afraid that if I stayed in my apartment alone that they would come for me, which they did. I went back once to get some clothes out of the apartment. The second time I went back to the apartment, it was sealed off. While I was standing there, my neighbor, who opened the door and just pulled me into their apartment, told me that they had come for me with bayonets or rifles. And he told me not to come back at all. I didn't. That was the last time I went to the apartment.

Through the influence of Kurt's boss, he was able to get his mother released. She also worked for a factory that did uniforms and I think that was in her favor, uniforms for the soldiers. She got her job back. And I lived with them. I was in hiding. They all three went off in the morning and I was alone in the apartment. And I really had to be very careful to make any kind of noise. I would never put on a shoe, and I would let the water run really softly, so that neighbors couldn't hear that somebody was in the apartment.

And then one day, I was still in bed, which was mid-morning, because that was really the only thing I could do in order to really keep quiet, there was a knock at the door. It was more than a knock, it was really a banging at the door. I knew right away that that wasn't a friendly neighbor knocking at the door. And there was no place to hide. In Germany you don't have closets or anything like that, so the only thing I could think of was I crawled under the bed. And just in time, because as I landed under the bed, the door was opened. They just broke it down.

It was the Gestapo with two Jewish men who were working with the Gestapo. I don't think they volunteered for that, but usually these were people in mixed marriages, they had Christian wives, and in order to save their hide they took jobs like that, just arresting other Jews. They looked around and didn't see anybody. I always felt, if they had been just a little bit smarter, they could have felt the bed, it was still warm. But they didn't. The Gestapo left and left orders with these two Jewish guys to wait until people came home and to tell them to get ready to be picked up maybe the next day.

While these two men tried to repair the door, or just put it up again, I couldn't stay under the bed, it was just not possible. So I came out. And they were very surprised to see me. I got dressed and then spent the day with these two men. One kept saying, "Do you have a place to go to?" And I really couldn't think. I might have gone to one of my aunts, but I knew I couldn't stay with her. But the other one didn't want to let me go. That was it.

So I stayed. In the meantime, one of the neighbors had called my mother-in-law to tell her what had happened, that the door had been broken into and that the Gestapo was there. She was convinced that they had arrested me, and she called her two sons to tell them. So when they all three came home in the evening, they were quite surprised to still find me.

We did get an extension. We were not picked up the following day. I think we had a few more days, but that was all. Because of the influence of Kurt's boss with the Gestapo, he could not save us from it, but he arranged for me to be deported with them, which got me to Theresienstadt. Otherwise I would have gone straight to Auschwitz like everybody else.

It was in June 1943.[18]

---

18 The Nazis closed all remaining Jewish organizations in Berlin in June and deported most of their staff to Auschwitz. Kurt and Sonja were deported on June 30, 1943.

Kurt: We were picked up from our house by truck and were shipped to one of those transit camps. They were synagogues and school buildings where people to be shipped out were just assembled and were pushed off. Grosse Hamburgerstrasse was one of those camps.[19] We stayed there two or three days. It was a Friday night. During this Friday night service, I had a guitar, a lute with me. I conducted services for the people. And we were singing. Later on I will point out that my singing ability helped in many, many ways. It gave us strength and, well, I'll come back to this later.

We were led on foot to a tramway. We had one rucksack, one bundle, that's all you were allowed to have for your belongings. By tramway we were driven to the Anhalter Bahnhof. There we were placed into regular trains, not cattle cars as later on. Those were real trains. As upset as we were, this wasn't too bad.

I'd like to shift back one moment. At the beginning of the Polish campaign in 1939, a dear friend of mine, a non-Jew, Walter Kleinhammer, went to war and came back from Poland after one month. He had already gained a leave of absence because he was a superb soldier. He had all the insignia and plaques and medals you can imagine, was a high-ranked officer. He came to my street. I was just leaving the house. I see him and immediately withdrew. How could I endanger this man? He was not allowed to speak to a Jew. He made it a point to motion me to him and told me, "Kurt, I have seen things which are beyond description. Leave, there is no choice for you, you have to try to get out at any cost as immediately as possible." And he himself said, "I don't even know how to live with this myself." A week later, this man had to go back to the front. One week after that, his parents, who lived in the same house, slipped through my door a little notice. Their son had been killed in action by the bullet he was looking for. This man was not a Nazi. So there are some of those also.

I just wanted you to know that at this moment I had no reason to doubt this man's testimony. Of course, I couldn't whisper a word of it to any of my friends or relatives, so I had to try to push it out of my mind somehow. Normally you speak to people. But with this burden I had to live, and even when we went now by train to Terezin, I still didn't want to believe it. I had pushed it a little bit out of my mind.

---

19 The Jewish old age home in the Grosse Hamburgerstrasse was one of the locations where Jews arrested during the *Fabrikaktion* were held.

Theresienstadt/Terezin

There was no place on earth like Theresienstadt. Its combination of genocide and culture was unique among the thousands of camps and ghettos created by the Nazis. Within the walls of the old Czech castle, Jews were starved, beaten, humiliated, always aware of the next transport east. Yet the inmates made music, created art, produced magazines, and taught children to write poetry. Most Jews deported to Theresienstadt were later killed in the gas chambers at Auschwitz.

The Terezin fortress was built at the end of the eighteenth century, 30 miles north of Prague, taking its name from the former Austrian Empress Maria Theresa. It became a prison in the nineteenth century. In November 1941, the Gestapo turned the walled city, which they called Theresienstadt, into a transit camp for Czech Jews. In all, 75,000 Czech Jews were sent to Theresienstadt, most of whom were transported within a year to their deaths in ghettos and killing sites further east.

Reinhard Heydrich, Nazi master of the former Czechoslovakia and leading organizer of the "Final Solution," suggested using Theresienstadt as a "settlement" for German-speaking Jews whose sudden disappearance might cause uncomfortable public questioning. In his report on the Wannsee conference of leading Nazi officials in January 1942, Adolf Eichmann, Heydrich's subordinate, explained this effort to camouflage the Holocaust: "It is not intended to evacuate Jews over 65 years old, but to send them to an old-age ghetto— Theresienstadt is being considered for this purpose. In addition ... severely wounded veterans and Jews with war decorations (Iron Cross I) will be accepted in the old-age ghettos. With this expedient solution, in one fell swoop many interventions will be prevented."

On May 27, 1942, Czech resistance fighters blew up Heydrich's car. Even before he died a week later, the first transport of Berlin Jews was shipped to Theresienstadt. Between June and October, 45,000 more "privileged" Jews from Germany and Austria arrived in Theresienstadt. Theresienstadt became a weapon of deception about the nature of the Holocaust.

Starting in October 1941, the Jews of Berlin were gradually deported east. Jews working in factories for the German war effort, like Sonja's parents, were initially spared, but they were rounded up in the so-called *Fabrikaktion* (factory action) in February 1943. Along with 5,000 other Jews, they were sent to Auschwitz. By May 1943, Nazi authorities declared the Reich to be *judenrein* (free of Jews), although this was just another of their lies, as there were still nearly 20,000 Jews left in Germany. Most had non-Jewish spouses, and thus were treated differently by the Nazis, and about 6,500 had gone into hiding. When Kurt and Sonja were arrested in June and sent to Theresienstadt, they were among the last Jews in Germany.

More than one-quarter of Jews deported from Berlin went to Theresienstadt, about 15,000. Not everyone sent to Theresienstadt was "privileged." The ghetto administration requested additional nursing staff, and a group of nurses from the Jewish Hospitals of Berlin and Vienna were arrested and sent to Theresienstadt in March 1943. Among them was Gerda Schild, 21 years old, whose mother was killed in Riga and whose sister was killed in Auschwitz. She was certified as a nurse by the ghetto authorities and worked in their nursing home.[1]

The most remarkable feature of the Theresienstadt ghetto was the cultural production by the prisoners. The concentration of hundreds of prominent cultural figures and the Nazi desire to use Theresienstadt to divert attention from the mass murder of Jews created a unique flowering of ghetto culture. Kurt tells of the developing musical culture after his arrival in June 1943. There were four concert orchestras, as well as chamber groups and jazz ensembles. The famous Prague conductor Rafael Schächter gathered a male and female chorus, and managed to perform Smetana's "The Bartered Bride" 35 times, and a Verdi requiem 15 times. The composer of the children's opera "Brundibar," Hans Krása,

---

1   See interview with Gerda Haas by Margery Goldberg, Holocaust and Human Rights Center of Maine Oral History Project, Auburn, Maine, July 8, 1987; transcribed by Megan Goggins, Nicci Leamon, Steve Hochstadt, Sarah Rigney, Cyrille White. All other interviews noted in this book were part of the Holocaust and Human Rights Center of Maine Oral History Project.

Gerda Schild Haas was born in Ansbach, Germany, in 1922. Her father was the town's Jewish butcher. In 1938, Jews were expelled from her school, and she had to go to school in Berlin. In 1939, her family was forced to move to Munich. Her father was able to get to England in 1939. Her mother was deported to Riga in 1941. In 1943, Haas was deported to Theresienstadt, where she worked as a nurse. In early 1945, Hass was sent with 1,200 Jews from Theresienstadt to Switzerland. After Haas was reunited with her father in the United States, she graduated from Bates College and became a librarian. In 1985 she helped found the Holocaust Human Rights Center of Maine.

and the set designer had already been deported to Theresienstadt when the piece premiered in 1942 in Prague, performed by children from the Jewish orphanage. By 1943, virtually the whole cast had also been sent to Theresienstadt, and Krása recreated the score for the available instruments. "Brundibar" was performed 55 times in the ghetto.

Fritz Taussig, an illustrator from Prague, led a Graphics Department of 20 artists, who created posters for the SS showing the physical development of the fortress into an internment camp for tens of thousands of prisoners. He also secretly drew pictures of the deplorable conditions, some of which were smuggled out. When this was discovered, Taussig and other artists were sent to Auschwitz.

The Austrian artist Friedl Dicker-Brandeis organized art classes for hundreds of children while she was in Theresienstadt from 1943 to 1944. Before she was deported to Auschwitz, she gave two suitcases with children's drawings to Rosa Engländer, one of the teachers in the girls' dormitory. Four thousand drawings by 600 child artists were saved and are now housed in the Jewish Museum in Prague.

The irrationality of the Holocaust and the continuing uncertainty of the Nazi murderers about what they were doing to Jews are illustrated by the deportation of 1,260 Polish children from Bialystok to Theresienstadt. When the Bialystok ghetto was liquidated in August 1943, the remaining 30,000 Jews were deported to their deaths in Treblinka, Majdanek, and Auschwitz, except for these children. In Theresienstadt, they were housed in newly constructed barracks, and taken care of by about 50 doctors, nurses and teachers. A few months later, in October between Rosh HaShanah and Yom Kippur, all these children and their caregivers were sent to Auschwitz and immediately murdered.

The most famous incident in the history of the ghetto, the visit of the Danish Red Cross in June 1944, illustrates the deceptive purpose of Theresienstadt as a "retirement home" for German-speaking Jews, the ability of the Nazis to adapt to unforeseen circumstances, and the opportunities of outsiders, nevertheless, to interfere with the process of the Holocaust.

When the Nazis tried to round up the Jews of Denmark for deportation in October 1943, the great majority were saved by a determined popular operation to ferry them to safety in Sweden. But nearly 500 Jews were captured by the Nazis in Denmark and sent to Theresienstadt. The Danes did not accept deportation as the final word, and insisted, uniquely in Europe, that the Danish Red Cross have access to the prisoners. After months of sending packages and demanding access, the Reich Security Main Office, in charge of the whole camp system, agreed to a visit. They told the Theresienstadt administrators to prepare the ghetto.

An elaborate and deadly hoax was created. Theresienstadt was "beautified" with paint and gardens; the residents performed "Brundibar" and played soccer, and Paul Eppstein played the role of "mayor." An integral part of this cleaning up was the deportation of about 7,500 Jews to Auschwitz to reduce crowding. Much to their discredit, the three Red Cross representatives did not penetrate this thin veneer, and apparently left thinking that Theresienstadt actually was a "model city."

The hoax worked so well, that the SS decided to broaden the audience by producing a documentary film a few weeks later, entitled "Theresienstadt: A Documentary from the Jewish Settlement Area," to prove that rumors of genocide were false. A German actor and director, Kurt Gerron, was enlisted to direct and produce the film. Musicians, like the jazz group "Ghetto Swingers" and the child actors in "Brundibar," were forced to perform. The SS controlled all aspects of production and then performed its version of cleaning up after the filming was over. The Ghetto Swingers, the "Brundibar" performers, and Gerron himself were put on trains to Auschwitz. Eppstein was shot. In September and October 1944, more than half of the remaining prisoners in Theresienstadt were deported to Auschwitz. Among them were Kurt and Sonja, and Kurt's brother Henry.[2]

The Danes had been duped, but their concern was not ineffective. Although most Jews who entered Theresienstadt were deported to Auschwitz, none of the Danes were. The Danish authorities, in the name of King Christian X, eventually secured the release of the 423 surviving Danish Jews, who were put on trucks hired by the Swedish Red Cross and brought back to Denmark in April 1945, two weeks before the camp was turned over to the International Red Cross.

Heinrich Himmler, in charge of the entire system of mass murder, recognized by late 1944 that the war would be lost to the Allies, and he began tentative negotiations with Swiss officials about the fate of Jewish prisoners. Himmler hoped to save himself by using Jews as hostages. After $1.25 million was deposited in Swiss banks by Jewish organizations as ransom, in February 1945 the SS transported about 1,200 Jews from Theresienstadt to Switzerland. Gerda Schild and her best friend, also a young nurse, were among those who volunteered for this transport, accepting the risk that it might be like

---

2   Henry Oertelt has published his own memoir of the Holocaust: Henry A. Oertelt and Stephanie Oertelt Samuels, *An Unbroken Chain: My Journey Through the Nazi Holocaust* (Minneapolis: Lerner Publications, 2000).

all the other transports, a free ride to Auschwitz. Only when they arrived in Switzerland were they sure they had made the right decision. This was a final deception organized by the SS, sending to freedom the healthiest, best dressed prisoners of the camp system, the inmates of Theresienstadt.

That was not the end of the Holocaust. The final transport of 117 Jews from Berlin to Theresienstadt was sent in March 1945. Between March and May, 1,100 Hungarian Jews and 1,000 Slovak Jews arrived there. In the three weeks before Theresienstadt was liberated, another 15,000 prisoners on death marches from Buchenwald and Gross-Rosen camps doubled Theresienstadt's population.

When Soviet troops entered Theresienstadt on May 9, they found about 30,000 prisoners.

Holocaust journeys of Sonja and Kurt Messerschmidt

Sonja: I don't remember the trip to Theresienstadt to be terribly uncomfortable. I think it was still a passenger train. And we were with our families, we had a little food, because we took it with us. In a way, it was almost a relief, because you had feared this moment for so long, you had been in terror. It had happened, and now let's see how we go on.

I was not thinking in terms of being killed, being tortured. These things never even entered my mind. We had been hungry for years, so being hungry didn't scare us. Going to work or being made to work, we have done that, so that didn't scare us either anymore. So it wasn't too bad. We arrived in Theresienstadt in the dark, and I thought it was very pretty, what you could see. There were small houses, narrow streets, it looked not scary at all.

We were immediately separated, men and women, as we arrived there. My mother-in-law and I, of course, I call her my mother-in-law, we were not married at the time so she wasn't, but we were put into an attic of a barracks. We were sleeping on straw, terribly, terribly primitive. I was only in my teens, it wasn't so bad, but for her it was most uncomfortable. I don't know how many people we were together in the room. Just one next to the other. No privacy and no place to put anything. And it wasn't the cleanest place either.

Then in the morning as we got up, it wasn't so pretty anymore. It was dirty and terribly crowded. But it wasn't terrifying, at least not to me. In time we were all put to work and I had a much easier job than I had while I was still in Germany. I worked in an orphanage in their sewing room, since I knew how to sew, and we repaired their clothes. I met a girl there, she worked with me, we went to school together. I hadn't seen her in years, even though we lived in Berlin. That's a big city. But that's where we met again, and we worked together.

Kurt: We arrived in Terezin. We could keep the few belongings we had. They took my lute. I will describe the arrival at the barracks I was assigned to. Huge attics with cross beams and millions of fleas, bedbugs, and other insects of all kinds, which is discouraging, but you don't think too much about this at the moment. There was a young man in our group, very sensitive, very small in stature, very white face, half alive, very spiritual appearance, who was desperate. And his will power broke down to a point that this is the first really shocking thing

I experienced even in lovely Theresienstadt. The next morning, this young man had died from the bites of the insects all over, the whole body was completely red, and he had died.

So we were then very, very careful and tried to continue living. Got slightly different locations with bunk beds and straw. And got food, very, very minimal, but excellent in taste. I had made up my mind, whenever entering a camp, the thing the Nazis want us for, if for anything, would be work. As long as you were able to work, they would find a place for you. So I always volunteered for the hardest things there were. This wasn't too hard, but I had to work outside of the ghetto, digging trenches for the waterworks, and after work I was able to do a few other things. And I did plenty of them. I don't think I needed much sleep then at all.

A few days after my arrival, the lute was returned to me, because they had heard that I was a cantor and singer. Terezin was a propaganda camp. This was a camp that Hitler created to show the world how well he treats Jews, so they had to show a few things. There was a coffeehouse, you could get some stamps and you could attempt for a cup of coffee. Some people entertained, and I was one of them, used the lute and sang Yiddish folk songs, entertaining people.

Then all of a sudden, there was a quartet of people. It was a double quartet who had arrived months before me, and they knew liturgical music and sang all kinds of classical stuff. This was wonderful for me. I was a cantor. I introduced myself to them. I knew all their music. And we started conducting services. This was not objected to, because they had to prove they that really meant what they said, this is a special camp. So we conducted services during the summer out of doors, only on Friday nights, and during the winter in very small attics which were crowded to bursting, because if anybody had reason to pray, it was us.

Sonja: A typical day was just going to work in the morning and coming home, whatever is home. We were moved to a different place. I ended up in a one-story wooden structure that they had put up because they had run out of other housing. It was brand new when I moved in. We were crowded in bunk beds, but at the time it seemed a little brighter and cleaner. Pretty soon we found out it was just infested with bed bugs, to a point where you couldn't sleep in it. We would take a blanket and sleep outdoors.

Food was scarce, but the food was cooked by the Czechoslovakians, who were very, very good cooks. It was tiny little portions, but whatever we got was very tasty. They performed miracles. We had a little dish and we had to stand in line, and they just put it in. In the evening you could get together with friends who were living in different parts of the ghetto. Kurt and I could see each other in the evening.

We did get married in the ghetto.[3] You had to be twenty-one to get married without permission, and I was nineteen. Even there they insisted, to make it legal, I had to have a guardian. I found a guardian, a Czech man who was a kind of a privileged citizen of Terezin, so that was all legal. He was somehow more privileged than we were. He had enough food. It was sent to him from the outside.

It was a religious ceremony, which we recognize to this day, that is our anniversary. We were married by a rabbi and he didn't care about, you know, your citizenship. I think the whole ghetto was there. Somehow everybody knew there was going to be a wedding, and the streets were lined with people who said, "Mazel tov, Mazel tov." It was almost like in a *shtetl*.[4] And of course there were many, many people in the hall to witness. It was a lovely wedding.

And it was a lovely wedding, and this Czech man actually provided some food which Kurt's mother cooked for a little celebration, but we were very few people for that. It was held in a great, great big hall. It was one of the *Kaserne* we got married?

Kurt: Yeah, A16 is the number, I know the building. I have a map of Terezin where I can locate every place where you lived, where my mother lived, where we lived, it's all there.

Sonja: It wasn't a big feast. As a matter of fact, we did have quite a bit. My guardian took care of that, I mean, he supplied it and my mother-in-law cooked it. And it was just before *Pesach*.

Of course we had to get married again after the war, for the Germans, they still wouldn't recognize it. We have a certificate, but it's meaningless to us, I don't even remember that date.

---

3   Sonja and Kurt were married in April 1944.
4   Jews in eastern Europe, especially in the Soviet Union, had been forbidden to live in cities for centuries, and gathered in small towns in the countryside, which were called *shtetl* in Yiddish.

Preparation was very little. There were plenty of rabbis in Terezin so that wasn't difficult, and we even had two choirs there. I had a brand-new dress, that was made for me, not a wedding dress, it was just a dress, and …

Kurt: Oh, it was beautiful, oh, it really was beautiful.

Sonja: Yes, it was a very nice dress, it was made by a very talented dressmaker in Terezin, she was a Czech woman and I worked with her. And she took it upon herself to make a dress.

For us, it was a big event. [laughs] It was an event as far as Terezin went, that there was a wedding. I don't know whether there were any others.[5]

You could get outside of the ghetto only if you were in a working unit that worked outside of the ghetto. We were totally cut off. We never saw anybody outside of the ghetto.

I remember the International Red Cross coming in once while we were there. They were announced weeks ahead of time and the main street was spruced up and people working on that project received a little bit more food, some extra food rations. It was in 1944.

Kurt: Terezin was marvelously organized. The railroad station was partially into the ghetto. The trains went every day out, in, out, in, constantly. And we knew it, because we heard the train whistles. Every night somebody from the Jewish administration came to the house elder, presented a list to him which he had to fill in. Each little block had to have ready for the next morning for transport a certain number of people. Quite a job. And we got used to it, because we knew that those house elders had to do it, so that nobody really rebelled too much against this.

We knew when trains came back that there were little messages to be found inside. The people who were sent away to wherever were forced to write postcards to the people who stayed back, to tell them how beautiful everything is, so they should volunteer to come. But

---

5   Other weddings took place in Theresienstadt. The sister of the creator of the underground newspaper was married there in 1943: Kathy Kacer, *The Underground Reporters* (Toronto: Second Story Press, 2004).

inside Terezin, inside the ghetto, it was quite well organized. The post-cards that came were written in code. And depending on who wrote them, we knew what the code was. Every seventh letter, then every sixth letter and so on, there was an arithmetical series. And we knew. These messages all said the same, "Don't come. Don't believe what they tell you. This is terrible, this is the end." So we all knew. Even after knowing this, we still kept hoping.

Let's talk about the good things of Terezin, because that is the puzzle. They call it now a concentration camp. We know it was a big sham. They tried to fool the whole world, and in order to fool it, they had to do things that were outrageously wonderful. So that's why we had this lovely food. My mother, who was diabetic, could get special food for diabetics, prepared especially. So how can you combine these things? I was allowed to conduct services. We performed operas, concert style but operas. We did "Carmen," Bizet has a Jewish background, Halevi, so this was allowed. Mendelssohn, they allowed the play "The Creation" to be performed. My brother and I sang in the chorus, I sang the solo part, the tenor solo part, in Theresienstadt, with the orchestra. The full orchestra came later, near the end when they were about to make that film. Brahms' "Requiem" was performed. There's a picture showing the rehearsal for "Messiah," we sang "Messiah," too. In that picture we could, my brother and I quite visible, there's no question that's us. So you see, when you see all of this, it must have been wonderful. The other side only we know. When you go to Theresienstadt today, what they show doesn't give you the right idea.

We saw people die, typhus and all these things were on the daily order, but on the other hand we had concerts, people entertained. A member of the Strauss family was there, a lady. There is a Jewish back-ground in the Strauss family. Nobody knows of it, but we knew it at Terezin because that one lady.

Of course as good as it was, they had to give it a special treatment when the Red Cross Commission came and we workers were put to work. There was a route mapped out where the Commission was led. They weren't supposed to go into any of the side streets to see all the misery. We had to paint the facades and women had to put out flowers. It was beautiful, what a show. But still, they couldn't keep it, because one of my dearest friends was from Denmark. He was an artist, he could imitate ladies' voices. This was one of his acts that he performed in Copenhagen in the Tivoli. Soprano, alto, tenor, bass, and he sang the whole "Rigoletto" quartet with his own voice, switching back and forth. He was a wonderful person. And he got very interested in my voice, too, because after the war he wrote me a letter, I still have it, he fortunately survived, and he said, "I just turned on the radio and look what we hear, that wonderful voice I heard somewhere else. It is you and you are alive." This man went to one of the Danish members of the commission and took him aside and showed him around. I know he did this. But somehow it was never published, nobody ever learned about it. So they knew about it, it was perfectly known.

Let me skip to the end of Terezin for me. The first two days of this month of Tishri are Rosh Hashanah, New Year, then a ten-day period of penitence, on the tenth day is the Day of Atonement, Yom Kippur, the highest holiday of the Jewish calendar.

On the first day of Rosh Hashanah in 1944, conducted the services, and lo and behold, we were left in peace. No whistles, the whistles stopped. Now we knew, through some outside information, which some people brought in via radio or somehow, that the Russian front was coming closer. So whenever anything of this sort happened, we were greatly encouraged. And the second day of Rosh Hashanah, not one whistle. The transports had stopped. I don't know whether I ever in my life repented and prayed as much as we did during these ten days. On Yom Kippur itself, I was given the honor of conducting the service with this choir in the Sokolovna. The Sokolovna was a huge, very modern, beautiful building which was, until a few months prior to this date, outside of the ghetto. For some reason, it was just before the High Holy Days incorporated within the ghetto. So we were allowed to use this tremendous hall, capacity of over two thousand or more people. The Day of Atonement was a very sunny day. It was warm, so we opened all the windows. And people were standing outside, because the whole ghetto was praying that this was it.

Yom Kippur is a day when you pray for twenty-four hours and you fast for twenty-four hours. Of course, the fasting was a very easy thing for us to do. On Rosh Hashanah the *shofar*, the ram's horn, is blown first to get people to pay attention, to take stock of yourself, repent, pray. On Yom Kippur, at the end, the ten days are over, the hope is that your prayers were answered. At the end of the Yom Kippur service, the great *shofar* tone, the *Tekiah Gedolah*, should give you hope. If you did everything right, this is your signal for forgiveness from on high and life will go on. Of course, we had prayed so desperately that we were only too happy to grab this signal as the intended sign of hope. The *shofar* was blown by a very, very old gentleman. He had been the cantor in Berlin, and when I knew him he was very tall in appearance, white hair, Cantor Levy. He was then in his high seventies. The man stood up and blew the *shofar*, and it was beautiful. We all started to almost inhale the sound. Suddenly, I shudder when I remember this moment, mingled in with this beautiful sound was a sound slightly off key. At that moment the whistle blew, the transports resumed, and the very next morning, my brother and I were on the transport to Auschwitz.[6]

Many people broke down completely, lost every faith. I don't know how I did it. We were numb. But I must have taken the other road, not to lose faith. How else would I have ended up continuing as a cantor and leader of worship? I cannot explain it. There are many things I cannot explain.

---

6   Yom Kippur lasted from sundown September 26 to sundown September 27, 1944. The next day deportations to Auschwitz, which had not taken place since July, resumed. Kurt was deported on September 29. He is listed as one of the "lecturers" in Theresienstadt in Elena Makarova, Sergei Makarov, and Victor Kuperman, *University Over the Abyss: The story behind 520 lecturers and 2,430 lectures in KZ Theresienstadt 1942–1944* (Jerusalem: Verba Publishers, Ltd., 2004).

Auschwitz

Auschwitz has come to represent the Holocaust in public understanding. That is a mistake. Auschwitz was unique among thousands of concentration camps.

Auschwitz was one among six death camps scattered across German-occupied Poland, where about half of the 6 million Jews killed in the Holocaust were industrially executed. For three years, Auschwitz was the deadliest place on earth. Between the end of 1941 and the beginning of 1945, over one million people, nearly all Jews, were killed in a few square miles outside the Polish city of Oświęcem. It was the first, and by far the biggest of these camps, but also with the largest number of survivors. While most people who arrived in Auschwitz were killed within 24 hours, many thousands were employed in industrial slave labor for giant German firms.

After the German defeat of Poland in fall 1939, about one-quarter of Poland was annexed to the Third Reich, including Oświęcem, which was renamed Auschwitz. The Nazis developed plans to replace the Polish and Jewish population of the newly conquered territories with ethnic Germans. About half of Auschwitz's population was Jewish, and immediately 1,000 Jews were deported east. Heinrich Himmler, in charge of an enormous resettlement policy, decreed that the entire territory of Poland which had been annexed to Germany must be cleared of Jews by March 1940.

This ambitious goal could not be fulfilled, and instead Himmler decided in April 1940 that a concentration camp should be established in the former Polish army barracks at Auschwitz to hold enemies of the Reich, namely Poles and Jews. Thousands of local residents were evicted to isolate the camp area. Soon the vision for Auschwitz expanded into a giant production site, using slave labor. Vast areas of surrounding farmland would be drained, and concrete would be produced from sand and gravel deposits. The German chemical producer I. G. Farben decided to build a factory to make synthetic rubber. Soon construction was underway on the largest concentration camp complex in Europe.

Every aspect of the development and functioning of Auschwitz demonstrates careful planning. Himmler visited Auschwitz in March 1941, as it was being constructed, and in July 1942, when he observed the operation of the gas chambers. He ordered the expansion of Auschwitz to hold 30,000 prisoners, the building of a new camp at Birkenau, about 2 miles from Auschwitz, for up to 100,000 Soviet POWs, and the construction by Auschwitz prisoners of a factory for I. G. Farben.

The first arrivals at Auschwitz in May 1940 were German criminals designated to act as functionaries within the camp system, the *Kapos*. In June the first transport of 728 Polish prisoners arrived. By early 1941, there were over 10,000 Polish prisoners, both Christians and Jews.

In June 1941, the camp began to function as a collection point for a much broader area, as political prisoners from Czechoslovakia arrived. After the sudden invasion of the Soviet Union in June 1941 resulted in millions of Soviet prisoners of war, they became a major potential labor force. In October 1941, 10,000 Soviet POWs arrived at Auschwitz. Within 3 months, 8,000 had died of overwork, cold, malnutrition, and disease.

At the same time, the end of 1941, the Nazi leadership came to the decision to murder all of Europe's Jews. During the summer and fall of 1941, special military units of the SS, the *Einsatzgruppen*, shot hundreds of thousands of Jews in the USSR, including over 33,000 outside of Kiev at Babi Yar on September 29–30. Carbon monoxide gas had already been used since January 1940 to kill over 70,000 disabled Germans. The physical difficulties of mass shootings, and the psychological effects on soldiers, convinced the Nazis that an industrial process based on gas chambers would be a preferable means of the genocide they were planning.

Zyklon B, a poison gas used to kill insects, was first used at Auschwitz to fumigate the barracks in July 1940. In September 1941, a new use was found: about 900 Soviet POWs and 250 others were killed in a makeshift gas chamber at the main camp, demonstrating that Zyklon B could be an efficient weapon of mass murder.[1] Two temporary gas chambers were built at Birkenau, which began operations in March 1942. In August, planning began for four major gassing facilities, to be constructed by German firms. They opened in the spring of 1943, after which Birkenau became the largest mass murder site in history.

---

1   A separate camp, called Auschwitz II or Birkenau, was built starting in October 1941, with much greater capacity for mass killing.

After the Wannsee Conference in January 1942, the transport of Jews from all over Europe to Auschwitz began. The first transport from Germany arrived in February; all were immediately killed in the gas chamber. Thousands of Jews from France were sent to Auschwitz beginning in March, from Slovakia in April, from Holland in July, from Belgium and Yugoslavia in September, from the Czech lands in October, from Norway in December.

In 1943, German Roma and Sinti were sent to Auschwitz, and housed in a special "family camp," which eventually numbered 20,000 prisoners. Another "family camp" was started in September 1943 for those deported to Auschwitz from Theresienstadt.

Auschwitz was more than a killing center. It embodied all of the Nazis' ideological war aims. Hundreds of thousands of prisoners were selected for work at the various factories, which represented major German corporations seeking cheap and expendable labor. I. G. Farben made synthetic rubber, Siemens made electrical parts for airplanes, and Krupp made armaments at Monowitz, a major sub-camp of Auschwitz, where Elie Wiesel and Primo Levi worked.

The historians at the Auschwitz-Birkenau Memorial and Museum estimate that one of every five Jews who arrived were selected for labor, registered, and given a numbered tattoo. Most of them died before the end of the war. The great majority were sent immediately to the gas chambers.

Auschwitz also provided German doctors and scientists with endless human specimens for a series of gruesome experiments. Josef Mengele was the most famous user of human beings for his research. After arriving at Auschwitz in May 1943, Mengele used the daily selections of newly arrived prisoners to seek out twins, his favorite subjects for experiments. Other SS doctors tried out methods for mass sterilization, such as x-rays and the injection of chemicals into women's uteruses. The pharmaceutical company Bayer tested drugs on inmates.

The most intensive period of killing took place from March to November 1944, when nearly 600,000 Jews were murdered, over 2,000 per day for 9 months. The ghettos at Łódź and other Polish cities were emptied. From May to July 1944, 430,000 Hungarian Jews were deported to Auschwitz. The number of Hungarians who were selected for work, as opposed to immediate death by gas, is uncertain, but may have been as high as 100,000. One survivor from this period, who arrived from Hungary in July and was shipped out again for slave labor three weeks later, is Judith Isaacson, who eventually settled in Maine.[2]

---

2   Isaacson's memoir, *Seed of Sarah* (Urbana, IL: University of Illinois Press, 1990), has been translated into Hungarian and German.

As the Hungarian Jews were being murdered, the Red Army advanced to within 150 miles of Oświęcem. The death camp Majdanek was evacuated in July, and the Auschwitz authorities began to plan the evacuation of the camp, which began in September. Those preparations included emptying the special camps into the gas chambers: the Theresienstadt "family camp" in July and the Gypsy camp in August.

The doomed men who took the bodies from the gas chambers to the cremation ovens, the so-called *Sonderkommando*, understood the meaning of these actions and decided to revolt by blowing up the chambers of death. On October 7, 1944, they succeeded in partially destroying one crematorium, whose ruins still stand at Birkenau, and in killing three guards. After the revolt was subdued, hundreds of *Sonderkommando* men were executed.

Kurt and Sonja belong to the small minority who survived to tell about Auschwitz. When they arrived in October 1944, most of the killing had already taken place, and the goals of the SS had shifted. Desperate to stop the advancing Soviet armies, fewer prisoners were sent to the gas chambers and more were selected for slave labor in Germany to support the war effort. They spent less than two weeks there before being shipped off again to perform slave labor.

The final use of the gas chambers to kill Jews was in November 1944. Franciszek Piper used timetables of train arrivals combined with deportation records to calculate 960,000 Jewish deaths and 140,000–150,000 ethnic Polish victims, along with 23,000 Roma and Sinti, and 15,000 Soviet POWs.

Sonja: As long as the four of us were there, we didn't worry too much. But then Kurt and his brother were shipped out. Of course they didn't tell us they were going to Auschwitz. We were told they were going to a camp where they had to work, a work camp. And then afterwards they told us that women could volunteer to go also. I volunteered. My mother-in-law also volunteered, but they wouldn't take her.

I remember that the little food that I had, that they gave us for the journey, I didn't eat because I saved it, I wanted to give it to Kurt. When the train finally stopped, we were in Birkenau. We were told to get off the train and to leave our baggage, whatever we had, on the train, it would be brought to us later on. And then there was the SS, with dogs, and we were very bewildered when we got out. We were looked over, we were separated old and young as well. We were told to also separate, women and children should go to one side.

I had been traveling with a young woman who had two small children. One was three and one was an infant. So I had helped her with these, mostly with the three-year-old, most of the trip. As we got off the train, I held onto this child, because she was busy with the baby. They were told that the women with children would not have to work, they would go into a much nicer place where they would be cared for. And I had this little three-year-old on my hand. Suddenly I decided to let go of him and to tell his mother, "You better take him." I don't know to this day what made me do it, because they never asked you, "Is this your child?" They just assumed you have a child on your hand, it is yours. I let go, and she took the child. And that saved me at that time, because they went straight to the gas chamber, we learned of that later. I would have been one of them.

So then the next thing, we were taken to a place where we had to undress totally and our heads were shaved and any hair on your body was shaved. Then we were taken to a shower room. And then we were given some clothes, it was just handed out, so I don't think I had any underwear. If I had, maybe a pair of panties, that's all, and a woollen dress, a navy-blue dress, I still see it. And it actually fit and it looked nice. And some wooden shoes. No stockings, nothing. And then we were herded into barracks.

Kurt: The arrival in Auschwitz was an unbelievable shock. We were still in our civilian clothes, and we looked out of the window and there were people with those striped uniforms. When they took their hats off, their heads were clean shaven. All of the things I had doubted and didn't want to know, all of a sudden it was crystal clear. This was Auschwitz-Birkenau. Now you began to live from hour to hour, from day to day. And each hour to hour, each day to day through all the Auschwitz days was a miracle. Many miracles happened. I believe in miracles.

We had to leave everything in the train, had to line up. Left, right, we went through all of this. The eternal standing in line begins now. I could see, all of a sudden, what up to this point I had only smelled. The stench of burning flesh was unbearable, but you couldn't miss it. I could see huge flames shoot up to heaven. I'd never seen anything like this. So it was all obvious and all very clear to me, and I had to recuperate from this first impression.

Everything had been taken away from us. We had been given the striped clothes and wooden shoes. But they were very kind to us. It shows again the diabolical intent. They didn't give us stockings, but they gave us pieces of prayer shawls which we were forced to use instead of stockings. A prayer shawl is something very sacred to an observant Jew. They knew where to hurt you, not just physically. So you had to start fortifying yourself, not against the physical things that might happen to you, but against the psychological. And this was even more shocking than anything else. But we had to do it.

So we stood in line in this new outfit and everything, clean shaven. There was a guy sitting next to a pail full of red paint and he had a brush. Everybody who got through there was given a vertical line down his back. While we're standing in line, I notice that ten people in front of me, there was all of a sudden a big stir, a big to-do among the people who were standing in line there. Somebody was given a whole design, a whole fence was painted on him, horizontally and vertically, a whole gate. A lot of screaming. I had no idea why. I found out the next morning.

We had an impossible night. Pushed into one of those barracks. Couldn't sit down. We tried standing, it was impossible to sit down. This barracks was probably meant for horses, only little openings along the roof on both sides, and in the middle a walkway, elevated, maybe it was where they put water in for the horses. One of those *Kapos* was walking back and forth with a whip, whipping constantly. How we physically lasted through the night, I'll never know. But this is a minor thing, a very minor thing.

Next morning, the daily order was standing in line, being counted over and over again, on the *Appelplatz* they called it. At this point, the SS wasn't there yet. The *Kapos* by themselves got us ready for the final inspection by the SS, who came a little later.

A little further away from me there was again a big to-do. The guy who got this gate painted on his back had been recognized by the painter as one who had acted as a traitor for the Nazis. He had sent the entire family of this man to Auschwitz. Then there were a few more who recognized him. On that morning the justice of the camp prevailed. This man was, without using any weapons, trampled to death in five minutes or less. And, you know, I agreed. Horrible as it was, I was the one who sings classical songs and enjoys fine literature, I had to agree. It's something I hoped I would perhaps later on overcome, and I did, but it took a long, long time. So this was a totally new way of life, or I'd say, of dying.

Sonja: We were herded into barracks where there are ten or twelve on a slab of wood in three layers. All women. We had to lie down, if we wanted to sleep, like sardines. You had to mold yourself to the one who was next, and some would lie this way and some other way in order to fit on that slab.

There were constant roll calls. The minute you sat down, you were called to stand outside and be counted. You didn't feel like a person in that place. When we were counted, we were always counted by SS and the dogs. We had no idea what they were going to do with us. Every so often, they pulled people out, to us for no reason at all, and we never saw them again.

Once I left Theresienstadt and arrived in Auschwitz, there wasn't a soul I knew. They were all people I had never seen. And at that point you didn't make friends. You were so determined to live through this, that you really concentrated on yourself. At least, that's the way I felt. You would talk to people. We talked about families. We talked an awful lot about food, we gave each other recipes that we had in our head. Maybe it satisfied our hunger. But you didn't make friends.

I saw the smoke coming out of the chimneys. And this might sound very strange, but I still didn't believe it. I did not want to believe it. It's just too horrible to believe you're in a place where you are burned. So I believed all of this much later, not then, not while I was there.

Kurt: The second night, we were in a barracks. It was completely flat cement floor. It was below freezing that night. There were big, wide openings instead of windows all around, so it was not possible for us not to see the flames shooting up. It drove some of the people there absolutely crazy. All of a sudden somebody screamed, animal-like sounds, and it was the end of that particular person.

It was so cold. We had some cocoa mats on the cement. We couldn't leave them there. We had to use those mats to block out the view of those flames, so we were lying on the bare floor. It became impossible because the *Kapos* went to work. They took pails of water, that night I'll never forget, and poured it on the cement. In the morning at least forty were frozen dead to the ground. They had many ways of doing those things. Things were happening which a pen would refuse to write down, and I leave some of it to other people who might be able to talk about it. I prefer at this point not to.

The food we were given was all rotten. It was water with a piece of cabbage perhaps swimming there, maybe even dirty water, put it that way. Once in a while we got potatoes. Any good potatoes, they had been taken by the *Kapos* and those who were constantly working there. For us, all that was left were potatoes of a kind you never saw. They looked like shrunken black prunes. If you eat it, you die, no question. My brother and I made up our minds, we are not going to eat. If we die, we'll die from hunger. That's what saved us, that we had that control over our bodies, that we would refuse to do this.[3]

---

3   The determination of Kurt and his brother to retain a semblance of "control over our bodies" by not eating rotten potatoes is an example of how they maximized their chances of survival. Of the 1,500 people on his transport from Theresienstadt to Auschwitz, only 157 were not murdered there, according to the online database of Holocaust victims from Czechoslovakia and in Theresienstadt: www.holocaust.cz/en/transport/52-el-terezin-auschwitz/page/39/.

Slave Labor

Even before the Nazis began to murder Jews, they forced them to do hard manual labor. In Germany and Austria as early as 1938, Jews without jobs were rounded up and forced to work in segregated columns. Sometimes the "work" was simply a form of public humiliation. Soon after the *Anschluss*, Viennese Nazis forced Jewish men and women to scrub political slogans off the pavement.

Eventually forced labor became a national policy designed to save money and replace the labor of the vastly increased number of men in the armed forces. For the six years from the invasion of Poland in September 1939 to surrender in May 1945, Germans forced Jews, and millions of other Europeans, to labor for the good of the Third Reich. Jews worked in construction, agriculture, forestry, and industry in more than a thousand ghettos and forced labor camps scattered across the continent. They collected garbage in Vienna, planted trees in Czechoslovakia, built the Autobahn in the eastern Reich, and sewed uniforms for soldiers.

They built the concentration camps in which they and their families were imprisoned, tortured, and murdered. These camps were sometimes under the jurisdiction of the SS, but many labor camps were outside of the SS prison empire. Jews worked for civilian government agencies, the Army, municipalities, and private enterprises. At one point, one million Jews were working for the Germans in Europe.

During the Holocaust journey of many Jews, slave labor seemed to present an alternative to death. The infamous selections at Auschwitz and other killing camps separated young healthy-looking men and women from the elderly, the infirm, and mothers with young children, who went straight to the gas chambers.

The "work" which spared Jews immediate death might be a living hell. Men who were selected for the *Sonderkommando* units at the death camps gathered dead bodies from the gas chambers, extracted gold teeth, and burned corpses, in the specially designed crematoria or in open fields. Although they might receive slightly better rations and housing than other prisoners, the *Sonder-kommandos* were routinely killed and replaced with new prisoners. Perhaps 20 *Sonderkommando* workers survived to offer the most intimate glimpse into the process of industrial mass murder.

As the war progressed, slave labor became a significant element of the Nazis' economic system. Enterprises saved millions of German Marks by over-working and underfeeding Jewish prisoners, drawing on the seemingly endless supply of victims when their workers became too weak or too sick to continue. Although the six death camps in Poland were kept hidden from public knowl-edge, Jews, Soviet POWs, and other eastern Europeans were visible to Germans on a daily basis across the Third Reich as they labored in fields or factories, or marched in columns back to their barracks.

Sonja's work on airplanes in Freiberg, a subcamp of Flossenbürg, was typ-ical of the desperate use of Jewish slave labor later in the war. During the win-ter of 1944–45, 1,000 female prisoners from Auschwitz, starving and freezing, worked at the Arado Aircraft Factory, alongside German civilian workers. But conditions were far superior to Auschwitz and survival was possible.

Kurt was sent in October 1944 to the cement factory at Golleschau (Goleszów in Polish), which had become the first of 50 Auschwitz subcamps in July 1942. He worked there for three months, until the approach of the Red Army in January 1945 led the Germans to evacuate some of the prisoners by marching them north through the snow to Gleiwitz, a distance of 50 miles. Another group of 96 Hungarian Jews were sealed into two cattle cars and sent on an aimless rail journey without food or water for over a week, until they ended up being left on a siding at Zwittau (now Svitavy in the Czech Republic). Oskar Schindler found them and had the cars sent to his factory at Brünnlitz, where those who survived were freed with the rest of Schindler's Jews in April by the Red Army.

From Gleiwitz, Kurt then passed through Sachsenhausen, north of Berlin, on his way to Ganacker in Bavaria, where prisoners also labored for the military. These constant movements were not unusual for slave laborers. Walter Ziffer went through at least seven different labor camps during the war, mainly doing construction, including helping to build the *Autobahn*.[1]

---

1   See interview with Walter Ziffer by Katy Beliveau and Paula Skolnick, Augusta, ME, April 14, 1987; transcribed by Steve Hochstadt, Nicci Leamon, and Cyrille White. Ziffer was born in 1927 and grew up in Cesky Tesin in Czechoslovakia on the Polish border. After the German Army invaded in 1939, his father became head of the *Judenrat* appointed by the Nazis. In June 1941 his family was deported. Ziffer went through seven camps, including

Sonja: I don't think I was there more than maybe ten days when there was another roll call, and we did not go back to our barracks. We were again put on a train, this time it was cattle cars, and we were taken out of Auschwitz into Freiberg, which is [Saxony].

It was another camp, it was just really a work unit. We were guarded by SS. There our group was working on airplane wings. I have always said that no plane ever took off that we worked on. We didn't know what we were doing and we were doing a terrible job. It was such a last-minute war effort that I don't know whether they really thought this would ever work.

It was winter, and I still had the same things on that I was given in Auschwitz, just a dress and those wooden clogs. We had to march from the barracks to the factory through snow. We may have been a couple of hundred at the most. We were forever hungry, because the food we got consisted of watery soups and a little piece of bread and in the morning some black water that was supposed to be coffee, and that was all.

We could hear the Americans' planes go over in broad daylight towards the end. All the Germans who were guarding us would go for shelter. We had to stay, of course, but to us this was music. There was no fear. We could have been killed by the bombs, but somehow that never entered our minds. We were just so delighted to know that, to us it was help on the way. And we could also tell by little things, for instance, again we had a German foreman. When we first got there, we watched him eat his lunch, which always looked very delicious, especially to us. He had salami and cheese and really nice-looking sandwiches. But towards the end there was no more salami, there was no cheese, he had a little jam on it. So little things like that. He didn't talk to us ever. I guess he was not allowed to. But he also didn't mistreat us in any way, he wasn't mean. He left that to the SS.

Life was pretty much routine there. We were not abused in a physical way. I once was slapped by an SS man, because we had to march by

Brande, Gross Rosen, and Waldenburg. He was liberated on May 8, 1945, and his parents and sister also survived. Ziffer left Czechoslovakia in 1947 for Paris, and arrived in Tennessee in 1948. He graduated from Vanderbilt University, where he converted to Christianity, and worked for General Motors for six years. Then he enrolled in the Graduate School of Theology at Oberlin College. He taught in France, Washington D.C., and Belgium. After returning to Judaism, Ziffer taught at the Bangor Theological Seminary.

him and it was cold, and this dress that I had had pockets, and I had my hands in my pockets. I wasn't even aware that I had my hands, but that was the only physical abuse that I ever experienced. We just went back to work and starved, little by little.

Kurt: I stayed in Auschwitz maybe just one week. I was fortunate. Those who were not eligible for work somewhere else would immediately perish, because Auschwitz was just an annihilation camp, a liquidation camp. That's what they called it proudly, that's all it was. But as long as you were able to work, and were lucky, of course, there might have been a chance.

Then came the big decision day, who will live, who will die, who will stay, who will go to another camp. Both my brother and I were lucky to be selected to be shipped out. Where were we shipped? To a camp named Golleschau, an infamous death camp. It was a quarry. We were actually shipped out for work, and we were selected because we looked as if we would be able to work. There was a truckload of perhaps eighty or ninety people. We stopped in front of this camp, Golleschau. On the other side, across the street, was another truck facing out, and we saw the people. They looked like the people you saw in those horrible pictures. No face left, the eyes, deep holes where the eyes would be, dead already. It was all clear. We might be, a week from that day, in one of those trucks which went back to the chimneys.

So knowing this, we went into this more than ever determined to outlive it. We were given a chance to pick our work, and I picked the heaviest work, the work in the quarry. There was a cement factory. So I worked in the quarry. My brother was very, very fortunate. He is a carpenter, a very skilled one, and it so happened that at that particular day they needed a skilled carpenter. This was a factory that built, I don't know, beer kegs or bigger kegs of some sort. He was assigned to this, which was a miracle, and I went into the quarry. It had one advantage. I was in fresh air. Of course it was in the winter, and the winters in Upper Silesia are horrible. Frequently, I worked night shift. Our clothing was nothing. But somehow we managed.

This was a horrible camp. You may have started in the quarry, work in fresh air, work very hard. The moment you failed, you were not killed, they gave you other work. Attached to this cement work was a coal mine. Those people who couldn't do the heavy work anymore were sent to other heavy work into the coal mine, and the coal dust did the job on them. And it didn't take very long. Whoever was through with the coal mine was then shipped back to keep the circulation going. There was a constant turnover in this camp, they used up so many human lives.

We were forced to witness hangings. The *Kommandant* made it his business to describe in detail how the arms would get out of their joints and forced us to suffer doubly. Then people who tried to escape were brought back by the dogs and their bloody bodies were displayed. We had to witness it.

No matter what my situation in life was, I always either sang or hummed or remembered some melodies or composed in my mind. I had a *Kapo* who was a professional criminal. They had a green triangle. He probably had been in prison for murder or something like this, and he would have been sent to the Russian front. He was deathly afraid of that, so he was very happy to do his killing right here and then. And he was very, very good at it. When we marched, if anybody walked half a step out, he was shot on the spot. Dogs were not with the *Kapos*, but they had all the weaponry that was needed.

But a very strange thing happened. I had noticed that this guy had an irritable flicker in his eyes at certain moments. So there was some mental condition, that was very obvious to me. Whenever this happened, I knew he was just waiting to shoot somebody. And I timed it right. I was humming and he came by somewhat closer. I never knew his name. I hummed and he stopped and listened. He went off, but he came back again, I hummed a little more. It was around midnight. There was just one little coal fire burning. He said, "Stop everybody, take five." He allowed everybody to gather around the fire. Now, that was wonderful. We didn't know why he did that. He said, "You, sing." And, well, I sang something.

I sang a Yiddish folk song which I had sung in Theresienstadt, and I didn't even know how right this choice was, how this would do something to him. It was the story of a blacksmith who is called to war, and he says goodbye to his wife and family. Each night, the wife prays with her son for the safe return of the husband from the front. In the last verse, the rabbi enters the house and tells the wife, Esther, "Be strong, be tomorrow morning at services. You have to say *Kaddish*, the prayer for the dead. Your husband is dead." Then it concludes with a very

Jewish lesson, because the *Kaddish* prayer reaffirms your faith in God in the face of any adversity. Now that part didn't touch this one listener. But what moved him was the fact that somebody was called to the front. I had to sing this once more and went back to work. Then I found out that he was afraid to be sent to the front.

So whenever I felt that he hadn't done anything bad for a while, maybe the time is up for me to sing, I started humming. And, sure enough, at least four times a week or so, he called a big break for everybody in order to listen to me. I didn't hold back. My voice was part of my professional equipment. But I thought only of the moment, and I had the marvelous feeling that I was doing, with my voice, something very unusual. I was actually saving lives. And that gave me such a wonderful feeling that I felt, to use a biblical comparison, like young little David who played for King Saul when he was plagued by evil spirits. The experience in Theresienstadt, when all of a sudden my world ended and all the faith should have stopped, it came back, it gave me strength in a different way.

I guess I was very, very fortunate. My brother and I lasted in our positions. There are a few details which I will not mention. I may mention just one thing which was a change from the everyday business. For Christmas, even at that camp, for those who still worked, they arranged for a party. That party was attended by the *Lager Kommandant*, his guys and the dogs, and everything was very neat. They were sitting in the front row and we were allowed to perform. For this particular event, musical instruments had been imported from the main camp, from Auschwitz. So I got a guitar, and I arranged for my brother and myself a duet of songs. There were other instruments, a little orchestra performed then, too, and I had to become their musical advisor. So I got an extra piece of bread on that day.

I tell you what we were singing: "*Die Gedanken sind frei, wer kann sie erraten.*" "Thoughts are free, nobody can guess what we think. You cannot shoot them, you cannot. They live." And this song my brother and I sang in front of these Nazis with such verve and *élan*, you can't believe it. This was one way to fight. They didn't say anything, but it was obvious.

January 1945, the Russians finally were so close that we had to flee from our liberators. Horrible as it sounds, that's how horrible it was, because this was the beginning of the death marches. We were given one little piece of bread, a blanket, and set on march. We marched and marched. Snow that high. Nobody plowed any road for us, and whoever stumbled and couldn't get up immediately was shot. This was the idea of the whole thing. The machine gun was in back, had to be pushed by some of our half dead people. That's how it went for days. Food was exhausted very soon. We stopped in Gleiwitz, there was a machine factory, they pushed us in there. The machines were ice cold. We couldn't lie down, so we stood and leaned on these ice-cold machine parts for the entire night. And the next night were driven out again.

I remember scenes, there was one tall gentleman with whom I had tried to form a singing group secretly, had a beautiful voice. I had arranged some music in my mind and we rehearsed a little bit during the few spare minutes we had. He was standing near his father in the courtyard. His father couldn't make it anymore, so he tried to pull up his father, and he was crying, tears streaming down his face. In the meantime, the *Kapos* were there with whips and bayonets or whatever they had to drive us on. I just kept looking back. I had to witness this horrible moment. This young man saw his father killed, and he was pushed on. He didn't last much longer. He was a strong man originally, but this picture is unforgettable.

That same night, I started to hallucinate. I saw lights where there were no lights. My brother, fortunately, that night was in a little better shape than I. Normally, I was the one who was in better shape. And he got me going. I regained my mind somehow.

Then finally, by open cattle cars, we were shipped further north. We ended up north of Berlin in Sachsenhausen, it's a very infamous camp. It was a terrible winter. The van next to us was occupied by six or eight SS men, and they had an open fire going. They had their full uniforms and they were dressed and fur coats. Two of them died from that cold alone. We must have been superhuman beings, because when we arrived finally in Sachsenhausen, north of Berlin, when we were unloaded, we were standing and sitting on about forty bodies. They had died, but they couldn't be removed. It was the 29th of January, and on the 30th it was the anniversary of the takeover by the Nazis. There were the SS and all the dogs.

That very first night we were there, the Allies bombarded this camp with such vigor, it was music for our ears, of course, that we had again to flee the second time from our would-be liberators. They put us in a train, we were shipped south to another camp, Flossenbürg. Flossenbürg had been a POW camp for Russian prisoners. It was converted now to a concentration camp like Dachau, with the Russians as *Kapos*. They were the wildest, they were almost worse than the German ones. I remember, we were standing in line, we always stand in line being counted or something. The young Russian two steps ahead of me, facing the other way, for some reason I'll never know, he turned around, without looking at me, and just swung his *Faust* against this side of my face. And I think since then I have a problem there, this goes back to that. Then I hear him still say to the whole group, "Жиди," "Jews," "Жиди." So this Russian antisemitism, Nazis, they had this in common.

We were still together, my brother. My brother then developed already eczemas and inflammations under his lymph, it was just terrible. No doctor ever saw him. No proper care, there was no cotton, I think paper was the whole treatment. He was suffering terribly, and I remember the two of us had only one blanket, bloody, bloodied, it's dirty and everything, but that's all we had. And somebody stole this blanket from us. I went and stole another one for my brother. So would you absolve me?

We were in bad trouble, because there are either dead or living people, there is no in-between. Beginning in Sachsenhausen we had to face a commission daily, who had to decide who is still able to work and who can be shipped off. So I made it my business, since he was suffering, that I always walked in front of him and I put myself together, old military style, and marched in front of him, didn't dare look back. Every time after we got through, I looked, ah, still there. This was our daily experience. And really, he had to make almost superhuman efforts to walk straight.

Then a few days later there was one of those selection processes again, and there he did not pass. There was a guy sitting with a small paintbrush, red paint, and each person passing by received a mark on his forehead. We didn't know what it meant, but we could tell after a while, because we were grouped accordingly. So all of a sudden I turned around, and that day my brother had a different mark on his forehead. There was no question what that meant.

I knew now we would have to be separated. And sure enough, the next day I was put on a train, and my brother had to stay back.

I never forget this, the looks of him, that expression, it's a terrible picture. I knew this had to be our last goodbye. It was just unbelievable.

I was shipped off to Ganacker, a small camp, nobody knew what that was, we were sure it would be somewhere near the front, where they use us as cannon fodder or something. There was nothing. This was just two or three airplane hangars, that was all, pushed us in. There was some straw there. They wanted to build a runway for their latest weapon, the *Wunderwaffe*, the V-2, to try to win the war in the last minute. Well, there was no food, there was no water. They finally shipped in some little water so we could wash our hands.

Two days later another group from Flossenbürg came, and there was one guy I knew and who knew me. He told me that my brother had suffered, the pain became so insufferable. He couldn't stand it anymore. He went down to the *Krankenbau*, to the infirmary, which of course nobody in his right mind normally would do, because in a camp like this you are either healthy or dead. Sick doesn't exist. There was nobody there to protect him, so there was no choice. And this practically confirmed it for me, because he couldn't have survived.

That's where he was lucky. He found somebody who liked him. The guy took care of him and gave him a job as a barber, cut the hair. It was really a marvelous thing he could do that.

There were certain times when they had to gather to be shipped off. On one day he was called to go and this other guy held him back, with the power of his arm, "You don't go. If you go, I kill you right here." That saved him again.

Then he was liberated, he saw the tanks coming. He finally got to Berlin. He could get back into his old apartment, they had to vacate this for him. The furniture wasn't there anymore.

Death March

As the German armies were pushed westwards by the Soviet Red Army in the fall and winter of 1944–45, Himmler ordered the evacuation of all camps in the East, trying desperately to eliminate evidence of the Nazis' genocidal activities. The SS destroyed gas chambers and buried bodies in mass graves. But the insane inhumanity of the concentration camp universe created by the Nazis continued right up to the day of German surrender, even as the camps themselves were abandoned. Guards rounded up many of the surviving inmates and marched them back towards Germany.

These journeys on foot during one of the coldest winters in modern European history have come to be called death marches, because the utter disregard for human life that characterized the camps continued along the roads. Inadequately dressed, with rags for shoes, without sufficient food or water, anyone who could not keep up was shot.

As columns of dying prisoners wound through little German towns, the locals urged them to move quickly, lest the oncoming Allies hold them responsible for war crimes. SS camp guards, Hitler youth, police, regular soldiers, and even civilians participated in killing prisoners in these last weeks of the war. While it is impossible to estimate the number of deaths on the road, probably a majority of the over 700,000 prisoners who were marched out of camps died of starvation, illness, or freezing, or were shot, on their way to yet another camp.

The largest death march originated at Auschwitz. On January 17, 1945, the final roll call counted about 65,000 prisoners. Beginning that day, 60,000 prisoners were marched out of the enormous camp complex, heading west. On that same day, the Red Army liberated Warsaw and was in the process of besieging Budapest, where eventually 119,000 Jews were freed when the city surrendered. The next day, the SS abandoned Chelmno after trying to shoot all the remaining Jewish prisoners. Only two or three survived.

In January 1945, Jews were marching all over eastern Europe. Emil Landau was marched to Gleiwitz, where Kurt also spent a few days, and then was put on a train to Buchenwald. Rochelle Slivka and thousands of other women were forced on the road from Stutthof towards Germany.[1] About 5,000 other prisoners from Stutthof subcamps were marched to the Baltic Sea coast, forced into the water, and machine-gunned.

One thousand Jewish women who had labored at a camp at Neusalz in eastern Germany were marched out of the camp on January 26, 1945, as the Soviet armies advanced to less than 100 miles away. By the time the column had traveled 200 miles to the camp at Flossenbürg 42 days later, only 200 survived. A week later, they were put on a train heading north toward Bergen-Belsen, a 300-mile trip which took 5 days.

At Neuengamme on the outskirts of Hamburg, about 12% of the 52,000 prisoners died in the first three months of 1945. Just days before the British army liberated the camp, another 9,000 were marched 35 miles to the sea, loaded on four ships and put to sea. The British RAF were bombing all vessels near the shore, and sank three of the ships.

Although only small remnants of prisoners eventually reached their destinations, the camps in Germany soon overflowed with new arrivals. Bergen-Belsen in northern Germany held 15,000 prisoners in December 1944. Over the next few months, 20,000 arrived from Auschwitz, and tens of thousands from other camps. Between January and April 1945, about 35,000 prisoners died there of disease and malnutrition, including Anne Frank, who had come from Auschwitz. When British troops arrived on April 15, they found 60,000 prisoners barely alive.

Sonja ended up at Mauthausen in Austria. Few Jews had been incarcerated there until thousands began arriving on trains from other camps. By the end of 1944, Mauthausen held over 100,000 prisoners. A list of those who died there, prepared with the combination of precision and prevarication typical of Nazi

---

1   Interview with Emil Landau by Sharon Nichols, Augusta, ME, March 14, 1996; transcribed by Nicci Leamon, Steve Hochstadt and Cyrille White; interview with Rochelle Slivka by Gerda Haas and Martin Margolis, September 1989, Augusta, ME. Emil Landau was born in Witten an der Ruhr in 1925, and attended a Jewish school in Herrlingen until 1939. In 1942 his family was sent to Theresienstadt, where his father died in 1943. Landau worked on the cemetery detail and in a bakery. In 1944 he was sent to Auschwitz, as were his mother and sister somewhat later. He was then selected to work in a refinery at Tsechowitz. In early 1945, Landau was forced on a death march to Gleiwitz, then on a train to Buchenwald, until the camp was liberated by the American Army. Landau recuperated in a Swiss hospital, and found his mother and sister in Bremen. He came to the US in 1946. He served on the Board of Directors of the Holocaust and Human Rights Center of Maine.

documents about the Holocaust, shows that 200 died per day in March and April.[2]

Although the German armies were in full retreat and the Nazi government in Berlin was collapsing, the elaborate processes of mass murder continued unabated.

Thousands of prisoners were killed as camps were abandoned. Two weeks before liberation, the SS guards murdered 3,000 prisoners in Mauthausen. A week later, another group of 33 anti-Nazi Austrian political prisoners were killed in the gas chamber.

On April 13, SS guards and local police in Gardelegen herded over 1,000 death marchers into a barn, which had been prepared with gasoline-soaked straw, and burned them alive. The next day, the US Army arrived in Gardelegen. Two days later in the Thekla camp, near Leipzig, 1,200 prisoners were evacuated and the remaining 300 were lured into a barracks building, locked in, and burned to death.

Even as Theresienstadt was being emptied, Jews from Germany were still being deported there. In January 1945, with the American armies just on the other side of the Rhine, SS headquarters ordered that so-called *Mischlinge*, people with one Jewish parent, prepare for deportation to Theresienstadt. In February, small groups of *Mischlinge* and Jews with Christian spouses were gathered in cities across the Third Reich and sent to Theresienstadt, even as the Red Army was only about 60 miles away. Manfred Kelman, who lived in Bremen and was classified as a *Mischling*, was deported there in December 1944 at age 16, and survived until the Soviet Red Army liberated the camp in May 1945.[3]

While much about the death marches remains uncertain, it appears that Jewish inmates were more likely to be forced out of the camps. Although a

---

2   A part of this list is reproduced in Steve Hochstadt, *Sources of the Holocaust* (New York: Palgrave Macmillan, 2004), pp. 214–17.

3   See interview with Manfred Kelman by Norma Kraus Eule and Paul Marcus Platz, Augusta, ME, November 10, 1987, transcribed by Steve Hochstadt and Cyrille White. Manfred Kelman was born in Bremen in 1928 of a Jewish father and a Lutheran mother, who converted to Judaism. Considered a *Mischling*, he could not attend the Gymnasium after 1938. On *Kristallnacht*, his father was arrested and later sent to the Warsaw ghetto, from which he returned in August 1939. In September, he was arrested again and sent to Buchenwald, where he died in 1940. Kelman continued in school and then worked in a soda factory in Bremen. In December 1944, he was deported to Theresienstadt. He was liberated by the Soviet Army on May 8, 1945, and returned to Bremen. In 1946, Kelman and his mother came to the United States. Kelman joined the Army, was on active service for 36 years, including the wars in Korea and Vietnam, and retired as a Colonel in 1983.

minority of prisoners at Dachau were Jewish, Jews were the majority of the 7,000 inmates who were marched south in April from Dachau 50 miles toward Tegernsee. They walked in daylight through the outskirts of Munich. Mostly Jews were marched out of Buchenwald south toward Flossenbürg, while non-Jews stayed in the camp until liberation.

At the end of their Holocaust journeys, after being separated for half a year, not knowing whether the other was alive, Kurt and Sonja were only 100 miles apart along the German-Austrian border.

Sonja: One day, we were again herded into cattle cars and we were on those for days. There is never an explanation. You don't know where you're going and why and what. I ended up in Mauthausen near Linz in Austria, after days without any food or water or anything. Sometimes the train would go very slow, there were people outside on the road who tried to throw bread into these cars, and the SS, at that point, let them.

As we arrived there, we were really scared, we saw a lot of people who we did not think were inmates. They told us that they were *Kapos*, but they told us that the SS had fled, they were not there anymore, so that nobody should be afraid, nobody would be killed. So when we arrived, we again were stripped and taken to a shower. We were so full of lice. The next thing I got to wear for the very first time, and that was already March or April of '45, was a striped uniform, because that was really a men's camp, it had always had only men there. Suddenly there were women, so we all got these striped uniforms.

Kurt: In southern Germany there were many of those death marches. Usually they started out at about nine hundred and ended up later on with very small groups. I can tell you only about the end of my own group. We were set on march again, and on the road somewhere now we came to the area, where we were approaching the Americans. There were always SS on motorcycles, back and forth, telling the camps to go on. Anybody who just stumbled was shot and if he wasn't dead immediately, then another shot to make really sure.

At one point they let us go. We didn't know what to do. I stayed one night with two others with some farmer, but he couldn't keep us, because he was still afraid. The war was practically over, but not completely, so they were afraid. So I decided we had to go. I spoke German so, and the other two didn't speak German, spoke a little Yiddish so we could understand each other. While we were walking, two SS on motorcycles caught us and they were discussing my future fate among them, where will we shoot them, because that's what they were doing, they were just rounding up people. I started talking to them. I talked an awful lot. But they didn't let us go.

With this group I finished up the death march, coming to Traunstein, a city twenty miles away from the Austrian border approximately, near Salzburg. On the way through Traunstein, I could sense that there was a change of attitude among the population, because they realized the end was here. Those who hadn't dared speak up until now, all of a sudden dared do it openly. We had the SS guarding us with their guns, rifles and everything. I still see, as today, the third floor in one house, big window, wide open. This wide-open window was filled by one tremendous woman, and she had a huge loaf of bread in her arms. And cut large pieces and threw it down to us, who hadn't eaten in days, knowing full well that this was a very dangerous thing for her to do. The SS realized it, too. But somehow the SS didn't do anything to her or to us. They fired wildly into the air. That's all they could do at this point, because they felt that the mood of the people was beginning to swing the other way.

During the last mile of the march we realized it had to be over in a day or two, so the populace realized that, too, and the SS became very uncertain, because the people were not happy with them anymore. It was about time. And they didn't shoot us anymore, because that's what they had been doing all along.

So we went on and they forced us into a little pigsty, which means the entrance was that high, meant for pigs only. We saw them drive out the pigs. We were in complete darkness. So the whole mess was there. Of course our sense of smell was gone, it didn't bother us. We probably didn't even notice it anymore. At this point we were completely unable to do anything, we were hardly able to put one foot in front of the other. We weren't really alive any more practically, at the end of our lives. I couldn't talk, we couldn't speak, we were completely gone. Talk, we couldn't, it would have been too much effort. There were sixty-five. They forced us into this pigsty. Now I realized, this is it, this nobody can survive. At least I wouldn't be able to. So somehow I waited for it to get light and I watched the SS guard. He was in a half-crouched position, so I could actually see his face. I heard planes in the air. Our senses were very, very sharpened. When there is no flesh on your bones, your senses are heightened in an unbelievable way.

It was April 30, '45. We could hear the planes and the tanks go by, they were on the way to Austria, the Patton Army and the French also. And so I watched, there were two SS guys, one was around the corner with a dog, and at the little entrance, high enough for pigs, there was the other guy with all his weaponry standing guard.

And I don't know what happened, but I watched the SS guy and I noticed that he showed a little uncertainty. I could have been wrong. I used to study people. Even when I was a young kid already I studied my neighbors and figured out, I wonder why I didn't go into psychology. And so I knew something was up, he wasn't sure. But all of a sudden I was sure of something. If I didn't get myself together, then I wouldn't survive the day or the night. I think if I had stayed another hour there, I would have simply collapsed and this would have been the end. So I got up suddenly, it was fairly dark, maybe the sun was rising. It was a snowy day, fresh snow was on the ground. So with the last effort I could muster, I got up, forced my way through all the people who were lying there in some form or other. And walked up to the guy, said something in German, I don't know what I said, but I forced myself to speak in a very clear voice, and really pull myself together. And without any further ado, I just walked by him, knowing he would not shoot. That's what he had done throughout the entire tour, constant shooting. Why I knew? I never know, but I was absolutely certain. I feel this may be my greatest moment of faith. I knew. May 1st, 1945, fresh snow on the ground, and I walked straight into the snow. Didn't have to worry about hiding myself because the snow would give me away, my uniform would give me away.

It was at the edge of the forest, walked into the forest, stayed overnight with a farmer. I never had a chance to meet the man again afterwards. He had very young SS with him. They were so young, they were listening to the radio, I could hear, and they just heard Italy is surrendering. They were crying, they wanted to go home to Momma. But still that wouldn't have stopped them to get a fling, an easy way to kill somebody, to do something for the *Führer*. But there was a sergeant who was a little older, and I did the thing that saved me before, I started talking in German. It so happened this sergeant was an educated man, and he realized that I was somehow educated, and he listened to me. He took me aside, told them not to touch me, gave me his jacket, and intimated to the farmers that I would stay overnight. I stayed in the stable with the cows. But it was very clean.

For three nights I walked. I ended up on top of a hill, I have the picture there. This was the *Gasthaus*, the inn, and the cemetery and the church. The innkeeper took me in.

I woke up in the middle of the night from horrible shooting, for about fifteen minutes. I couldn't explain it. I thought the war was over in this area, it was already May. In the morning I found out. The sixty-four other pigsty inhabitants were let go by the SS about two hours after I had left on my own. Townspeople told me later, it was very moving because they stayed together, they sang together, and started their march into their newly won freedom. In the middle of the night they came to a large farm across the road from where I was, and Ukrainian SS were in that farmer's home. All the Ukrainians had to see were the striped uniforms. With their machine guns immediately mowed all of them down. Two of them went into another direction and had the same fate, were also killed.

I went in another direction, I'm the only one who survived. I asked myself why. Never got an answer. The answer I had to give myself, because it placed some obligation on me. And I have tried to fulfill it by exercising my profession.

Much later I found out that there was somebody else who had left this pigsty even before me, who also had survived. He was much younger than I, and a few years ago he called me, and we are in touch now, too.

Liberation

The end was an anti-climax. For most who survived until the German surrender on May 7, liberation meant life, the end of the constant threat of murder. The Holocaust was over. But survivors of concentration camps were too exhausted, too sick, too hungry, and too disillusioned to realize the meaning of their new freedom. Judith Isaacson wrote that she was "too dazed to fully appreciate it."[1] Elie Wiesel described his limited thoughts when American soldiers arrived at Buchenwald: "Only of bread."[2] Emil Landau, also at Buchenwald, had gangrene, frostbite and typhus.[3]

The moment of liberation was not what the liberators expected either. The Americans who found Sonja and her fellow survivors in Mauthausen were, in her words, stunned. The chaos of death that liberating armies found in camps across Europe was unbelievable. In the summer of 1944, the Red Army came across the remains of the death camps in Poland: Majdanek, Treblinka, Sobibor, and Belzec. Even more shocking was the liberation of Auschwitz in January 1945, where 7,000 emaciated prisoners and a warehouse with 14,000 pounds of human hair were graphic evidence of years of genocide.

The US Army found its own horrors in Germany. On April 4, soldiers entered Ohrdruf, a satellite camp of Buchenwald. Thousands of prisoners had died there over the past few months, and most of those still alive had been shot by the guards just before liberation. Dwight Eisenhower, Supreme Commander of Allied Forces in Europe, heard about the gruesome scene of death and brought Generals George Patton and Omar Bradley to view the camp. Harry Blumenthal, a medic with the unit who arrived at Buchenwald on

---

1   Isaacson, *Seed of Sarah*, p. 116.
2   Elie Wiesel, *Night*, translated by Marion Wiesel (New York: Hill and Wang, 2006), p. 115.
3   Interview with Emil Landau.

April 11, said, "everywhere there were bodies."[4] Wiesel was one of 21,000 still alive in the sprawling camp.

Another gruesome scene was found by US soldiers at Nordhausen on April 12, part of the Dora camp system, where the Nazis had hoped to create V-2 rockets to win the war: 3,000 corpses in unheated concrete hangars. Warren Blackwell said, "It was just row on row on row upon rows, dead bodies, skeletal. Still had their skin on them. And some alive."[5] William Millar recalled that seeing Nordhausen was "one of the most ghastly experiences I think I've ever experienced."[6] The next day, American soldiers forced 2,000 townspeople to bury the dead in mass graves.

Two weeks later, as Bernard Cheney's unit approached Dachau, they found 30 boxcars filled with corpses. In the camp, 32,000 prisoners were still alive. Cheney said, "They were horrible specimens of humanity—like scarecrows."[7] By this time American soldiers began to understand the outlines of Nazi crimes, and at Dachau took a measure of revenge: US soldiers and former prisoners killed many of the captured German guards.

---

4   Interview with Harry Blumenthal by Sharon Nichols, Augusta, ME, November 4, 1992; transcribed by Steve Hochstadt, Nicci Leamon, Cyrille White. Blumenthal joined the Army while attending the University of Pittsburgh, and trained as a medic. His unit followed the Allied invading forces into Germany. In April 1945, he participated in the liberation of Buchenwald concentration camp near Weimar. He gave medical assistance to surviving prisoners and conducted the photographer Margaret Bourke-White through the camp.

5   Interview with Warren Blackwell by Donald Isikoff and Laura Petovello, Augusta, ME, December 11, 1992; transcribed by Steve Hochstadt, Nicci Leamon, Cyrille White. Warren Blackwell was born in Maine in 1925. At age 18, Blackwell joined the US Army and became a medic. He landed in France two months after D-Day. His unit fought across Belgium into Germany and in the Battle of the Bulge. He saw the concentration camp Nordhausen just after it was liberated. He returned to Maine in July 1945.

6   Interview with William Millar by Norma Krauss Eule, Augusta, ME, November 3, 1989; transcribed by Megan Goggins, Nicci Leamon, Steve Hochstadt, Cyrille White. Millar was born in Springfield, Massachusetts, and graduated from the University of New Hampshire. He went through Officer Candidate School and joined the 104th Timberwolf Division fighting in Holland in fall 1944. Millar was wounded in December 1944 and transferred to England. He rejoined the 104th Division in April 1945 and helped liberate the concentration camp at Nordhausen on April 11. After the war, Millar worked at Bath Iron Works for 31 years.

7   Interview with Bernard Cheney by Walter Taranko, Augusta, ME, July 10, 1995. Keith Waning was also with the 45th Infantry Division when it arrived at Dachau: interview with Keith Waning by Gerda Haas and Sharon Nichols, Augusta, ME, September 8, 1989; transcribed by Steve Hochstadt, Nicci Leamon, Cyrille White.

The largest number of survivors were found by the British army at Bergen-Belsen in northern Germany. On April 15, about 60,000 prisoners were liberated there.

Liberation did not mean life for all who had survived that far. The appalling conditions in vastly overcrowded camps left thousands on the edge of death when liberating soldiers arrived. Nobody was prepared to deal with tens of thousands of dying prisoners. The sudden availability of food posed grave dangers to people who had been systematically starved. The medical personnel and facilities of the liberating armies were inadequate to deal with thousands of sick prisoners. At Bergen-Belsen, about 14,000 died in the two months after liberation. At Mauthausen, about 3,000 died, and over 1,000 Theresienstadt prisoners died after the Nazis left.

Liberation was an end, but not yet a beginning. What now? Where to go? Who was left from family and friends? Survivors had no resources, no possessions, and no influence with the Allied armies. Resuming their pre-war lives was impossible: central Europe was a devastated landscape of occupied nations.

Even returning home was difficult and dangerous. Travel over a few hundred miles could take months. After years of absence, Jews were not welcomed back into their homes or jobs, occupied by others.

In Poland, Christian antisemitism led to the greatest tragedy of the postwar period, the murder of returning Jewish survivors. Alan Wainberg's family, after hiding successfully until the Soviet Army came in 1944, went back to their Polish home in Żelechów, along with about 60 of the nearly 6,000 Jews who had lived there before the war. But they soon left, afraid of what they had been hearing about Polish Christians killing Polish Jews who returned home.[8] Chaim Hirszman, one of only a handful of survivors of Belzec, gave testimony

---

8   See interview with Alan Wainberg by Gerda Haas, Augusta, ME, November 5, 1990; transcribed by Megan Goggins, Nicci Leamon, Steve Hochstadt, and Cyrille White. Alan Wainberg was born in 1937 in Zelekhov, Poland, south of Warsaw. In the fall of 1942, the Nazis began to deport Jews from his village, so his family hid, first in an attic, then in a hole under the house of a Polish farmer, where remained for nearly two years. The Polish underground AK discovered them and they had to flee. The family spent several months hiding in fields until the Soviet army liberated them in the summer of 1944. In 1946, Wainberg with his brother and sister left to try to get to Palestine, but ended up in Paris with his parents. In 1948 the family emigrated to Costa Rica. In 1949, Wainberg and his brother went to Detroit to yeshiva. They later returned to Costa Rica and opened up a store, Bazaar Detroit. Eventually Wainberg returned to the United States, went to college and graduated as an engineer. He moved to Maine in the mid-1980s.

to the regional historical commission of Lublin in March 1946, and then was murdered by Polish antisemites the same day.

The Polish city of Kielce has become the symbol of violent postwar Polish antisemitism. After about 200 Jewish survivors had returned to Kielce, an enraged mob, aided by local government officials, murdered 42 Jews on July 4, 1946. Other smaller outbreaks of violence claimed the lives of at least 300 returning Polish Jews. In the immediate postwar years about 120,000 Jewish survivors left Poland.

Sonja's story of her narrow escape from Soviet-occupied Austrian territory exemplifies the dangers faced by survivors even after the day of liberation.

Kurt: Next day, I could go on. I asked some people, they told me, "Go up there, there is the American government." On top of a huge hill, there was an inn, and a church, and at the entrance door to the gate there was one little piece of paper, Eisenhower's proclamation. This was America for me. It was an unbelievable moment. The innkeeper and his wife took me in.

I stayed in this inn. People nursed me not to full health, but to some degree. The tracks had been destroyed, there was no traffic, no transportation.

So I stayed now in Traunstein, too sick to go anywhere. And even if I had been well, I couldn't go anywhere because there was no transportation, you couldn't leave, anybody, anywhere. Of course I was listening constantly to the radio, Austrian radio gave through constantly search messages, the same notices you find all over the radio, I was listening for hours and hours. No result. I went to the American military government place in Traunstein, they couldn't help. They gave me finally permission, I could travel somewhere. But there was nothing yet. So the first freight train that went to Munich, to the capital, I was on, sick as I was. In the meantime, I had busied myself, I had acted as the interpreter for the villagers. First the French came through, I interpreted for them in French. Then the Americans came, I interpreted in English. Then I gave to the priest and his whole group a course in English, just to keep busy. But at the first train, I was on to look for my family, to Munich. I started looking as soon as I had liberated myself. Now starts something else, now starts the rebuilding process.

Sonja: The SS had fled. The Americans were very close, and they did come in within a few days. It was a wonderful, wonderful moment when they came in. But thinking back, I was not as excited and as jubilant as I thought I might have been. I think we were all numb. It was a wonderful sight to see them, but they were so stunned, especially when they saw women in there.

They didn't know what to do first for us. They set up soup kitchens, that's the first thing they did. With their kindness they killed a lot of people, because we were not used to food, especially not rich food or a lot of it. Some people just ate and ate and died. Thankfully, as hungry as I was, I wasn't capable of eating very much. They also opened the gates and told everybody to go out and steal whatever they could steal from the fields. So people went out and dug up potatoes and cooked them over an open fire. That killed them, too, just eating too much.

When they realized that there were women, they themselves went into the villages around the camp and took out of the stores whatever there was. There wasn't much, after all the war had gone on for years, but they went into homes, opened drawers, took out clothes, and brought them to us. So I had two sweaters suddenly, and I think a skirt.

I got quite sick. I had a high fever and had to be in bed, and I don't know whether I coughed. An American doctor came to see me, and of course he had no X-ray machine or anything, but just examining me he decided that he would like to send me to Switzerland. He assumed I had tuberculosis. But I didn't want to go. I said, "I can't go anywhere, I have to go back to Germany, I have to find my family." So he tried to persuade me, but there was also a language barrier, he spoke English and I spoke German. I could understand a little of what he said and he understood probably a little of what I said. But I didn't go to Switzerland. I stayed in Mauthausen for quite a while, because I really had no place to go. Some picked themselves up and just walked out. I didn't know how to go about it.

I figured anybody who survived in our family would try to get back to Berlin, and this is what I had in mind to do. In the meantime, the camp was taken over by the Russians. The Americans retreated and the Russians took over this whole territory. The Russians were not much nicer than the Germans to all of us, because to them it didn't matter if you were Jewish, not Jewish. You were German, and they hated us. They raped the women and beat up the men who were there. So

I locked myself in, and I remember a Russian soldier once came to the door and he banged and banged, and I was scared to death. But he went away. He did not break down the door.

I was very fortunate. One of the women I had known in Freiberg where we worked on the airplane parts, she had been in Theresienstadt, too, I didn't know her then. She had befriended one of the American officers while we were still in Mauthausen, and she left with him, the Americans went to Linz. When she heard that the Russians had taken over the camp and she knew I was still in there, she persuaded him to go in and try and get me out, which wasn't easy, because the Russians didn't let anybody out.

This friend of mine came with the American officer in a jeep, and they came to my door and said for me to leave immediately, to take as little as possible. I had little to take anyway. They put me into the jeep on the floor, covered me up with all kinds of blankets, and went back through the gate where there were Russians. The American officer spoke only English to the Russians, they didn't understand a word. He showed them some papers which they couldn't read, and they held them upside down, but he looked very official and he was in his uniform and they let him go, they just didn't know what to do with him. So then he just hurried out and I was out of the camp.

After we were out of Mauthausen, I could come out from under the blankets. They took me to an apartment where there were several other people who had also been in camps. We were all waiting. Quite often, there came buses from Germany, arranged by former inmates of other camps, who were looking for people to bring home. So I finally went on a bus that was going to Frankfurt am Main. I had never been to Frankfurt, but I wanted to get back into Germany and somehow find a way to get back to Berlin. By that time Germany was in zones, there was an English zone, a French zone, and a Russian zone. And Berlin was in the Russian zone, so that already was a problem. You could travel between the American and English zones, but you couldn't get into the Russian zone, so I had to find a way. Well, anyway, I was back in Germany.

Munich

Every Jewish family had been torn apart by Nazi persecution. A lucky minority had managed to escape Europe before the Holocaust began. Some had managed to adopt false identities or hide with sympathetic and brave Christians, like Charles Rotmil.[1] About 3,000 Jews hid successfully within the Third Reich, half right in Berlin. Some like Kurt and Sonja survived the camps and ghettos. Across central Europe liberated Jews began to search for relatives. As Sonja said, "Everybody was looking for somebody." In the case of Sonja, Kurt, and Henry, each thought the others were dead.

Millions of Europeans, not just Jews, but also many others who had been torn from their homes by war and persecution, now were placed into a new social category—displaced persons. At the end of the war in May 1945, there were about 11 million DPs, more than 8 million of them in Germany. About 700,000 were concentration camp survivors, but only about 75,000 were Jews, who were much more likely to die in camps than non-Jews.

Camp survivors owned nothing. Even their clothes were probably taken from others, who were now dead. One of the unexpected tasks of the Allied occupation forces was the care and feeding of DPs. Provision of food, shelter, clothing, and money for survivors was accomplished by a variety of organizations: Jewish charities, such as the American Jewish Joint Distribution

---

1   See interview with Charles Rotmil by Sharon Nichols, Augusta, ME, June 24, 1997; transcribed by Steve Hochstadt, Nicci Leamon, and Cyrille White. Charles Rotmil was born in Strasbourg in 1932. His family moved to Paris and then Vienna, where his father was arrested around *Kristallnacht*, November 1938. The family was able to leave for Belgium later that month, and then fled to France as the Germans invaded in May 1940. Their train was sabotaged and derailed, killing his sister and mother. Rotmil then lived with his brother and father in Brussels. In 1943, his father was arrested, and eventually deported to Auschwitz, where he was murdered. Rotmil and his brother were hidden in Catholic homes in Belgium for the rest of the war through a network organized by Father Bruno Reynders, who saved hundreds of Jewish children in this way. After the war, Rotmil and his brother emigrated to the United States to live with relatives. He earned a Masters of Fine Arts in writing from Vermont College and lives in Maine.

Committee, and the Hebrew Immigrant Aid Society (HIAS); the newly created United Nations Relief and Rehabilitation Administration; the Allied armies; and eventually the two new German governments.

Berlin had been home to the largest pre-war German Jewish community, but the capital lay in ruins and was located in the middle of the Soviet zone of occupation. As relations among the Allies deteriorated and the Cold War began, Berlin became less attractive to surviving Jews. Most congregated in the American zone in southern Germany, where the US authorities were sympathetic to Jewish desires for some voice in the political argument about what to do with DPs who could not go home.

Getting into the US was still very difficult, at least until 1948. The British tried to intercept those who illegally attempted to get to Palestine, as in the case of the SS *Exodus* in 1947, which was boarded and sent back to Europe by the British navy.

Postwar Germany did not offer a secure home for survivors, even those who spoke German. Hitler was dead, his government dissolved in defeat, and the Nazi Party was outlawed, but the racist ideas which led to genocide lingered in the German population. Although the Allied administrators in the four occupation zones used various methods to prevent former Nazis from holding positions of public trust, important men were able to hide or submerge their tainted past lives in both the Soviet and the Western sectors.

Surveys by American occupation authorities in the US zone showed the depth and persistence of the hatred of Jews: in 1946, 40% of respondents were classified as "antisemites" or "hard-core antisemites." Three years later, just after the founding of the West German *Bundesrepublik*, a national survey revealed similar results. In August 1947, 55% surveyed believed that "National Socialism was a good idea badly carried out."

Yet western Germany was more hospitable to Jewish survivors than Poland or the rest of Eastern Europe, where the Soviet authorities soon resumed antisemitic purges. About 25,000 Jewish DPs remained in Germany. They gradually recreated small Jewish communities in their new homes. But living in the homeland of Nazism was always a compromise.

Kurt and Sonja were unusual among the Jewish survivors in Germany. Only a small minority were from Germany; the rest originated in Eastern Europe, especially Poland. They did not live in a DP camp, because Kurt was able to find a job and housing in Munich. Like most survivors, though, they stayed in the American zone of occupation in southern Germany, rather than return to their native Berlin in the Soviet zone.

Sonja: The bus stopped in Munich in a home for the aged, and we had a nice lunch. In their foyer was a big bulletin board with all kinds of messages, everybody was looking for somebody. So somebody said to me, "Why don't you put a note on there, you are looking for your husband?" I said, "Why would he ever go to Munich? We have never been to Munich." He said, "It doesn't cost you anything." I said, "You are right." I put a note on, that said I was there and that I was going to Frankfurt am Main.

I stayed there for a couple of weeks. Frankfurt was in the American zone. Then somebody said that it was much easier for somebody to take you into the Russian zone to Berlin from the British zone. I took a bus to Bielefeld, which is in the British zone.

In order to get to Bielefeld I went to several other places, Germany was full of refugees, that's what we were. There were central locations set up where you registered, that you had come into the city, and they provided you with a place to stay, and some food and maybe even a little money. When you decide you're going to leave again, you go back to them and tell them, "I'm leaving and I'm heading towards Bielefeld." And that's the only way you could really find somebody, because these places existed and gave you the information you looked for.

There I lived in a hostel. It was full of people with the same story I had, and waiting for an opportunity for somebody to take you. You had to do this during the night, you really had to smuggle yourself into the Russian zone. While I was there, I found out that my brother-in-law was alive. I met somebody who for some reason knew that he had survived. But he told me that he was almost certain that my husband did not survive. So I wrote a letter to my brother-in-law, I can't even say where I addressed it to, maybe to my aunt whom I thought was still living there. He got the letter. He didn't know that I was alive, there had been no communication.

Kurt: Now I came to Munich and go up to find myself in the office of the *Jüdische Kultusgemeinde*, the Jewish community. The synagogue had been destroyed. They just had saved one little library room. There were lists, from all over people came looking for other people, so there were lists of survivors or lists of people who had been there and looked for this or that person. While I was looking through the names, in walks the president of the congregation, Dr. Spanier, and the communications officer of the radio station, Radio Munich, Sergeant Lehman.[2] I remember these two gentlemen very vividly. While I was looking, I couldn't help overhearing what they were discussing.

It was about five days before Rosh Hashanah, the New Year's Day. They said, "Well, the High Holy Days, we want to show the German public that Judaism survives. We want to put a big service on for them. How do we do it?" "Well," the sergeant said, "that's easy. I have beautiful records from America. We can put the record on, that's it." I heard this. I had to stop what I was doing. I went in. "Gentlemen," I said it in German, the American was originally from Germany, "I can't help overhearing what you're talking about. But I think you don't hit the right angle here. These American records don't prove anything. It so happens I am a trained musician and a trained Jewish cantor, who is a survivor. I am here just to look for my family, but I will be very happy to give you a service which will have authenticity for this particular situation." They got terribly excited.

I promised Dr. Spanier, "I will put a radio program together for you. If you give me a place to stay overnight and some music paper, and get some little organ, even a pump organ in here, and this pianist you just showed me, I will show him what to do, I'll write out everything for him." It was all set. My mind was very busy with finding my family, but doing such a good deed, having a chance to sing praise of the Lord after my liberation for a few survivors in Munich, this was more than anybody could ask for, so I could not say no.

I committed myself to conduct the Rosh Hashanah High Holy Day services for them in the little library room they had. But I said, "I need a place to stay overnight." No problem. A former Jewish home for the aged also served as a haven for returnees from concentration camps on a temporary basis. They phoned and the jeep took me there. Down comes Mr. Oestreicher, a little man with a goatee, probably about eighty years old, and said, "Herr Messerschmidt, I have heard you are the greatest." He got so excited. He said, "You just wait a moment, I go up and get your room ready." So he goes up the steps, the jeep leaves, and I am standing in this foyer. All the walls of the foyer were filled with

---

2   Julius Spanier (1880–1959) was born in Munich and became a children's doctor. He was a prisoner in Theresienstadt 1942–1945. After liberation, he returned to Munich, where he resumed his practice, served as President of the Israelitischen Kultusgemeinde in Munich, and was elected to the Senate of Bavaria.

little notes, who has seen this and that, if you have seen this and that call there, write there if you, and so on, these people looking for people.

While I'm standing there, looking, all of a sudden I see my name. I had never been in Munich, so who would look for me? Sonja Messerschmidt. It's very strange. Whenever I tell this story, I don't tell it often, I always think I have it under control. It's not possible. It was such an unbelievable moment. [pause] Yeah.

I found her notice. All right, that's when I learned for the first time that you had survived, and then she had left, her next place would be Frankfurt.

I went up to my room. I couldn't sleep, understandably so. In the middle of the night I ran down again, it had to have been a dream. It was true. Now I had a problem. Phones didn't work. I was committed to the services, and of course after this good news there was even more reason to go through with conducting a service of thanksgiving. They got for me music paper and I sat down and wrote down from memory about fifteen minutes of music with organ accompaniment and everything.

I did conduct the services for the congregation. Then I went back and went to the radio station and we did one service.

The last time I had seen Sonja was on Yom Kippur of 1944 in Theresienstadt, where I conducted the services, with choir and everything. The day after, we were deported. In the *Kol Nidrei* prayer, which is the introductory prayer to the Day of Atonement, we hope the coming year may be all for the good, "from this Yom Kippur until the coming Yom Kippur." And this also comes out absolutely letter perfect. At times, if I think of the things I went through and I experienced, I think it is fiction. But it is the truth.

Through the connection I had with the military government, they provided me with a jeep, courier took me to Frankfurt. I couldn't get anywhere else otherwise. She had left already, but again the system worked. They told me exactly where she had gone, so that's how I found out she's in Bielefeld. It wasn't easy to get there, but I had the good fortune to have that jeep. So they drove day and night. We went to many cities that were completely destroyed, there was no window left, and then there were others where there was not one window harmed.

Then I arrived in Bielefeld. I found my wife exactly on Yom Kippur 1945, so it has been, as one should say in the vernacular, in the cards.

So we found each other, what now? We couldn't go to Berlin, it was not possible. But we tried to get back to Munich, because that was the only address I had at the time. I had the connection with the radio offices, with the Jewish community, so that was the natural way to do it. It wasn't easy, because the trains were, people were hanging from the rafters and you couldn't get on. And I remember, one train would have been impossible to get on, but fortunately I knew enough English, so I could talk to the American who handled the baggage. I spoke to him in English and identified myself. There was room for baggage only. Well, that's why we could get in.

Sonja: We were baggage, too.

Kurt: So we got back to Munich, and we stayed there in the home for the aged, which turned out to be the beginning of a five-year career which I had with Radio Munich.

Sonja: That's the place where I left the note, and that's where we moved in. For quite a while. Munich is where our daughter was born. So we really started a new life there, knowing that we weren't going to stay there forever, but it was a beginning.

We lived there for five years. In Munich in November of 1945, I was still too young to be married without permission of somebody, so I got another guardian, this time a lady who had been in Theresienstadt and went back to Munich. When I told her of my plight, that I wanted to get married and there was nobody I knew who would take me on, she said, "I'll be your guardian." It really was just a formality. We just had a civil ceremony by a Justice of the Peace to make it legal. But I can't even tell you the exact date, because we don't recognize that as our anniversary.

We were under the protection of the Americans, who made sure that we had what we needed. We really were, for the first time, privileged. We were given an apartment of former Nazis. We had more food stamps than the Germans did. We recuperated. Our daughter was born in Munich in '46.

We didn't think we would live there forever. The American doctor had been right, because they did discover that I had tuberculosis and I was sent to sanitarium [laughs] and slowly recuperated after that. And then there was the birth of our child, so we felt we are starting new. For quite a while, I still had the hope that somehow my parents had survived. That was foolish to even assume that there was a possibility, but there was always a glimmer of hope. My two aunts in Berlin had survived, so there was a little family, even though one of them I never got to see again, because I never went back to Berlin and she was not well enough to travel.

Entertaining displaced families waiting to be relocated, Hanukkah 1946

Leading first commemoration service at Dachau after liberation

Kurt: Once we went back to Munich, I didn't know whether we would emigrate to America. So there was still something we had to try to do while we were in Munich. Through the radio connection which I had, I could be employed by the radio station, and the Jewish community was interested enough to make me their Chief Cantor. And so the connection between the Jewish community and the radio station provided some basis to live. It wouldn't have been enough the very first year. That's where HIAS had to help us.

With Radio Munich, I had a program of fifty minutes of religious services every Friday night for five years, until practically the day of my emigration in 1950. The radio choir, a choir of forty professionals, were delighted to sing our Hebrew music. They did a beautiful job without any pay. This was after their hard-working hours. They were just wonderful to do this. I considered this quite a mission. And it became a tremendous education for the general public. The letters, I wouldn't call them fan letters, because that's not how I would have liked to be looked upon, but the letters were unbelievable. Some I have with me. People ran home Friday night at a quarter to eight to hear this broadcast.

But I wanted to do a little more, because I was a teacher also. So I figured, well, why shouldn't I apply for a job to the school *Verwaltung*, school department in Munich. I filled out all the applications, everything, and no answer, no answer.

I developed quite a reputation in Munich. I have letters from all over Europe, even as far from Israel, in response to the radio programs.

After I was a very well-known soloist at the radio station, a Cantor, I took part in interfaith concerts. We had meetings with the *Weih-bischof*, the Cardinal of Munich, planning an interfaith concert. And I took part in that, I was the Jewish part. My radio choir was not available for this concert, so the cathedral choir volunteered. This was the Catholic aspect. And now they needed a Protestant, and so they brought the Leipzig *Kantor*, the successor of Bach after hundreds of years, so we had all three religions combined for this interfaith concert. Was a tremendous event.

And so it would have been a career, but our daughter spoke to one of the other little girls that lived in our house, and that other little girl told us and her what their teacher had taught them. They didn't have enough teachers that had not been Nazis, and so they de-Nazified quite a number of them. And believe it or not, this teacher taught exactly the

Nazi ideology to this generation. Which means that we have to leave. The career would have been possible in Germany, but that was the final decision. So we decided very quickly, but it took a long, long time.

We called my brother, who was in Berlin. I don't know to what degree he had planned to emigrate, at one point he must have thought about it, too, but he eked out a living in Berlin. I made it clear that we are going to emigrate. And that caught fire with him and he immediately got active. From Berlin, for him, it was easier to get out, quicker than me, so he left Germany before us. We had planned earlier, but I was happy that that could be arranged for him.

In addition to this, I sang all kinds of other things. But this has become my main concern. That's why I ended up as a full-time cantor here in the States now.

Maine

When Nazi antisemitic policies accelerated after their seizure of power in 1933, German Jews who tried to leave the country looked overwhelmingly toward the US as their preferred next home. Although restrictive quotas and prejudicial immigration procedures made it difficult for Jewish families to get visas to the US, nearly 100,000 German-speaking Jews managed to enter the US before World War II began.

At the war's end, there was little alternative but to remain in Europe. The American quota systems, which had kept thousands of potential Jewish immigrants out of the US before the war, continued in operation. In Congress and in public opinion, there was little sympathy for Jewish survivors. A Gallup poll of December 1945 showed that 37% of Americans wanted the number of immigrants from Europe reduced to less than before the war. But President Truman and a number of eastern Democrats in Congress kept pushing to liberalize immigration policy. The Truman Directive in December 1945 allowed organizations, not just relatives, for the first time to issue affidavits. The Displaced Persons Act of 1948 allowed 200,000 DPs, not just Jews, to enter over the next two years. Further liberalization came in 1950.

From a trickle of survivors right after the war, tens of thousands came annually in the years around 1950, then the flood slowed by 1954. Eventually about 100,000 Holocaust survivors entered the US between 1945 and 1952. Nearly three times as many went to Palestine, then Israel after its founding in 1948. Each destination offered unique hopes and opportunities.

Most new Jewish arrivals stayed in New York, home of 40% of American Jews. The most important task was finding housing and job. National Jewish organizations such as the United Service for New Americans cooperated with local organizations, like the New York Association for New Americans, to find these necessities.

Kurt's and Sonja's first experiences in New York were typical for these newly arrived refugees. They received financial help from an American Jewish welfare organization. They looked for work. Many refugees dispersed to other Jewish communities, joining relatives, finding jobs, and gradually assimilating into the freest society they had ever experienced. They raised American families.

And they were not well understood by American Jews, because they also remained survivors. Their persistent accents reminded others of their foreign origins; their nightmares reminded themselves of their traumatic pasts. Americans, both Jews and non-Jews, only gradually realized that these newcomers were not ordinary immigrants, but survivors of genocide. It took decades before Americans developed respect for the character of survival and the value of testimony.

The only long-term stability in the lives of Kurt and Sonja Messerschmidt occurred in Maine. After years of uncertainty, stretching from the early 1930s through the early 1950s, including the necessity to remake their lives in a new place over and over again, they eventually found a comfortable and welcoming home.

During the past 30 years, survivors, like Kurt and Sonja, have increasingly been asked to talk about the Holocaust to Jewish congregations, to school children, to college classes. Their memories have been recorded as historical documents through large interview projects, such as Steven Spielberg's Shoah Visual History Foundation, and small ones, like the HHRC's effort to interview all survivors and liberators living in Maine. By putting their lives on public display, Kurt and Sonja teach us what we must know.

Sonja: We decided that we would never be happy raising our child in Germany. First of all, there is always the fear that anything could happen again there. As a matter of fact, Kurt had a job offer to come to Holland and I said, "If I leave Germany, I'm going to go far away. I'm not going to go to Holland." I don't want to be that close, because Holland was not safe, far from it, during the war. Coming to America really was the best thing we ever did. Coming to America was our decision. We came as displaced persons, without money, but with a lot of hope.

Kurt: We left Munich in 1950, left Bremerhaven on the eve of Independence Day, came to New York. That is also significant. That's when our independence began.

Sonja: We spent about a year in New York. We were taken care of by HIAS, who set us up first in a hotel for a short while, and then helped us find an apartment, helped us with just enough money to pay our rent and food. We had actually what we needed. And then Kurt, of course, tried to find a job and did.

Kurt: I came to New York. It was announced in the *Aufbau*, the German-Jewish reconstruction paper, "The famous *Oberkantor* of Munich is coming to conduct our High Holiday services." The congregation was Beth Hillel, 182nd Street in uptown Manhattan. This was a congregation consisting of former Munich citizens. They had their old Munich rabbi still with them. So this was offered to me and, well, can I say no? This was very, very nice, it was lovely. But it had a very, very bitter by-taste, because they hired me for the High Holidays. That is when normally a Cantor's full-year position starts. They had a Cantor, they didn't need me. So it was nice, I could sing with the choir, wonderful, but after this it wouldn't have worked out.

Fortunately there was a fellow student of mine who was studying also to become a cantor and teacher in Berlin, Ehrenberg. He was the Cantor in the Jewish Tabernacle, which was at the time in 161st Street, it's now somewhere else in Manhattan, uptown. When he heard that I arrived, he got in touch with me immediately and realized what my situation was. He got in touch with a little congregation in New Jersey, the Lyndhurst Hebrew Center. He said that they needed a rabbi, a cantor, a teacher, an office boy, for a little congregation, all American congregation. So I ended up in Lyndhurst, New Jersey, becoming their Reverend, that's the title. Which was fine, it was a wonderful experience for me. Not sufficient for what I wanted to do.

We lived in the Bronx. I had to go there by subway and bus, through the Lincoln Tunnel and back and forth. Well, it wasn't ideal, but it was something. I took care of the school, I was teaching, I put on plays with them and everything, they were very happy with me. The pay was something they could easily afford, it was very, very, very little.

But they were very generous on Hanukkah. [laughs] I love to tell this, because that's what they did with newcomers, even Jewish people. They'd take advantage of later newcomers, figuring that they didn't have to suffer through their early years. That I was in a concentration camp, of course, they didn't realize, of course, I couldn't blame them for that.

Hanukkah. The chairman of the board was a guy from Russia. [laughs] He was a big contractor, he built all the new homes in all of Lyndhurst. His trademark was they had floods in all of his cellars, which means the lovely little temple, they had also a basement, where I was teaching, but it should have been renamed the swimming pool.

On Hanukkah they took care of the whole situation. They gave me a check for ten dollars or something, very minor, but then the gift. Would you be able to imagine what they gave me for a gift? I got a pair of galoshes. [laughs]

I don't know how I reacted to it. I think I was dumbfounded. I didn't say anything, because it's unbelievable, it was unbelievable. There was no question I wouldn't stay there, anyway. Because this was not satisfactory, it was nice that I could have the classes I had for myself and the children, I could handle things and there was no problem at all, and they enjoyed, we had a *Simcha Torah* celebration. Eva, Evie, our daughter was with us, so I took her for the celebration. During that celebration the children march around with the *Torah* and flags, and on top of the flags they have an apple. This is tradition. So they all walked around, and my daughter, knowing not this particular tradition, did only that part she was familiar with. She ate her apple. [laughs]

What I should say in retrospect, this one year in Lyndhurst was a wonderful experience, because from the first *Shabbat* on, I had to deliver a sermon in English to this all-American congregation, and I did it and I'm very proud. I have my sermons still bundled up in one of my bookshelves. So this was a wonderful experience. They wanted to nail me down, they had already arranged for a little house, apartment, and showed it to me. No, I wouldn't be buried there. I'd rather be buried here, that's very lovely.

Sonja: New York was not to our liking. Even though we met old friends and some relatives there, it wasn't the kind of life we would have enjoyed, even then. And it was a lot nicer than it is now.

Kurt: Maine, how did that happen? So I had to apply to various places and theological seminary. I got an interview at the hottest day of the year with the president of the congregation and the then rabbi, Temple

Beth El in Portland, Maine, Rabbi Bennett, he's passed on since, wonderful person, and had a wonderful meeting. I played for them my music, sang for them, and we clicked immediately.

Sonja: Portland, or Maine rather, reminded us a little bit of Bavaria, you know, the landscape and the lakes and the mountains and the climate. And it seemed like a nice place.

We had another child in 1953.[1] He can run for President. [laughs] He is an American. One of them is so interested and has become very active in the group children of survivors, and the other one, it doesn't seem to affect her in any way. I can tell that neither of them was hurt by our experience. But one just takes it as a history lesson, while the other one is getting really caught up in it.

Kurt: There were so many things one has to be grateful for. From 1951 to 1985 I served as the cantor at Temple Beth El. In Portland we performed Bloch's "Sacred Service" with Portland Symphony and an eighty-voice choir from Beth El and Brunswick combined in 1972, which was a first for the state of Maine to hear this. I prepared the chorus and was a soloist, and the conductor at the time was Paul Vermel.

My brother was a trained joiner, cabinet maker, making fine furniture. He went to New York first. But at the time New York was overrun with newcomers, so they couldn't place him properly. In New York there was nothing for him, he could nail together egg cartons or something like this.

They offered him to go to Minneapolis and he was probably a little bit uncertain, but the way it worked out, this was the best thing that happened to him. So he went there, and there he had an offer to become a salesman in a furniture store, Cardozo, a very, very fine furniture store. They hired him for his knowledge of woods and this of course was valuable. But they found out that in addition to that he was a guy who knew how to talk to customers, who could be with people.

There was one insurance man of Prudential, who was a customer of theirs, who had to deal with him, who was so impressed with him that he said, "Well, do you like whatever you're doing, waiting for customers to come all day long?" He convinced him he should try to take

---

1 Michael Messerschmidt is a lawyer in Portland, Maine.

tests and to become an insurance man. He took the courses, and it was a few years, a few hard years he had, but he stuck it out, became very successful as an insurance man. He made a wonderful home for his family. After his retirement, then he started lecturing, this was a side thing, it became now the main thing after his retirement, and he enjoys this very, very much. He is very active in speaking and lecturing. He published his little book.[2] So I'm looking very much forward to see him again. We meet once a year in Florida.

Sonja: [I have nightmares] and it is more or less always the same. I'm always running and always trying to find a place to hide. There's very little time and no way of preventing anything. But the thing that makes it so difficult is that I'm trying to protect my children, and that is what is strange, because at the time I had only myself to worry about, no children.

Kurt: We are so happy that we came to Portland. And not only are we happy, we're happy with the fact that our children loved it, too, because we didn't have a chance to ask them, "Should we go there, would you come along, Evie?" No, it's all worked out. Evie went to Brandeis, Michael went to Harvard, they all came back to live in Maine. So I did the right thing, not realizing what I did then. It worked out very, very well for us. New Yorkers warned us, "You want to go up to Maine? It's cold. Not only the climate, but the people are cold, Yankees," you know.

It proved differently. I mean, we warmed up to these cold people very easily and very quickly.

And I just retired two years ago to a rather busy retirement. I don't think I should add much more. I think I've told you already much too much. And yet, not enough.

---

2   Oertelt and Samuels, *An Unbroken Chain: My Journey Through the Nazi Holocaust.*

Kurt and Sonja at home, Portland, Maine

Conclusion

The survival of a fragment of the Kolbelsky-Messerschmidt family is one remarkable Holocaust story among millions of family stories. Death and love during the Holocaust rarely turned out this way.

Kurt and Sonja were German Jews, whose experience under the Nazis was unlike that of Polish Jews or Hungarian Jews or even Austrian Jews. Their path toward death was drawn out over more than 10 years, while Hungarian Jews, like Judith Isaacson and Elie Wiesel, were swept up in a genocidal whirlwind between May and July 1944. Further east, the Jewish population of Kiev were murdered by shooting ten days after first encountering the German Army.

Kurt and Sonja don't teach us the Holocaust, but we learn from them about part of the Holocaust. And this book is not their whole story. At the end of his interview, Kurt said, "I don't think I should add much more. I think I've told you already much too much. And yet, not enough." There is the dilemma of the Holocaust interview—not enough for us, but too much for him.

Although Kurt and Sonja have been remarkably generous with their memories, revealing humiliating experiences they would rather not remember, we still want to know more. The feeling that we must know more, that we can never know enough, is the reason for this book. Every incident they tell could be described in more detail; the number of incidents could be multiplied over the lifetime of death and destruction that swirled around them.

We honor survivors, but we want something from them: their stories remembered precisely, told in detail, repeated for interviews, audiences, and school classes. We are happy when survivors like Sonja and Kurt can create normal lives, surrounded by life rather than death. Yet we ask them to go back into the Holocaust for our sakes and for our children, for history and education.

We have no right to make such requests. But our need is great. We are indebted to all the Maine survivors who sat for HHRC interviews, and to tens of thousands who have done interviews around the world. They have done much more than reveal their personal trauma. Collectively they have opened up the Holocaust to our understanding, revealing the policies and behavior that the perpetrators would rather have kept secret.

Kurt's and Sonja's stories are unique, but their pieces make the giant puzzle of the Holocaust a bit clearer. Humanity abandoned them for the years of their persecution. Now they offer humanity their stories, in the hope that reading them and thinking about them will help us to be better humans.

For that we thank them.

Sources

INTERVIEWS WITH THE MESSERSCHMIDTS

Messerschmidt, Kurt, by Katy Beliveau and Paula Scolnik, November 18, 1987, Augusta, Maine. Transcription by Megan Goggins, Nicci Leamon, Steve Hochstadt, Cyrille White.

Messerschmidt, Sonja, by Gerda Haas and Margaret Meyer, November 18, 1987, Augusta, Maine. Transcription by Kate Caivano, Megan Goggins, Steve Hochstadt, Nicci Leamon, Cyrille White.

Messerschmidt, Sonja and Kurt, by Steve Hochstadt, July 29, 2004, Portland, Maine. Transcription by Nicci Leamon and Steve Hochstadt.

OTHER HHRC INTERVIEWS

Blackwell, Warren, by Donald Isikoff and Laura Petovello, Augusta, ME, December 11, 1992. Transcription by Steve Hochstadt, Nicci Leamon, and Cyrille White.

Blumenthal, Harry, by Sharon Nichols, Augusta, ME, November 4, 1992. Transcription by Steve Hochstadt, Nicci Leamon, and Cyrille White.

Cheney, Bernard, by Walter Taranko, Augusta, ME, July 10, 1995.

Haas, Gerda, by Margery Goldberg, Auburn, Maine, July 8, 1987. Transcription by Megan Goggins, Nicci Leamon, Steve Hochstadt, Sarah Rigney, and Cyrille White.

Kelman, Manfred, by Norma Kraus Eule and Paul Marcus Platz, Augusta, ME, November 10, 1987. Transcription by Steve Hochstadt and Cyrille White.

Landau, Emil, by Sharon Nichols, Augusta, ME, March 14, 1996. Transcription by Nicci Leamon, Steve Hochstadt and Cyrille White.

Millar, William, by Norma Krauss Eule, Augusta, ME, November 3, 1989. Transcription by Megan Goggins, Nicci Leamon, Steve Hochstadt, and Cyrille White.

Rotmil, Charles, by Sharon Nichols, Augusta, ME, June 24, 1997. Transcription by Steve Hochstadt, Nicci Leamon, and Cyrille White.

Slivka, Rochelle, by Gerda Haas and Martin Margolis, Augusta, ME, September 1989.

Wainberg, Alan, by Gerda Haas, Augusta, ME, November 5, 1990. Transcription by Megan Goggins, Nicci Leamon, Steve Hochstadt, and Cyrille White.

Waning, Keith, by Gerda Haas and Sharon Nichols, Augusta, ME, September 8, 1989. Transcription by Steve Hochstadt, Nicci Leamon, and Cyrille White.

Ziffer, Walter, by Katy Beliveau and Paula Skolnick, Augusta, ME, April 14, 1987. Transcription by Steve Hochstadt, Nicci Leamon, and Cyrille White.

ADDITIONAL READING

Cohen, Beth B. *Case Closed: Holocaust Survivors in Postwar America*. New Brunswick, NJ: Rutgers University Press, 2007.

Friedländer, Saul. *Nazi Germany and the Jews, v. 1, The Years of Persecution, 1933–1939*. New York: HarperCollins, 1997.

Hitler, Adolf. *Mein Kampf*, translated by Ralph Manheim. Boston: Houghton Mifflin, 1971.

Hochstadt, Steve. *Sources of the Holocaust*. New York: Palgrave Macmillan, 2004.

Holian, Anna. *Between National Socialism and Soviet Communism: Displaced Persons in Postwar Germany*. Ann Arbor, MI: University of Michigan Press, 2011.

Isaacson, Judith. *Seed of Sarah*. Urbana, IL: University of Illinois Press, 1990.

Kaplan, Marion A. *Between Dignity and Despair: Jewish Life in Nazi Germany*. New York: Oxford University Press, 1998.

Oertelt, Henry A., and Stephanie Oertelt Samuels. *An Unbroken Chain: My Journey Through the Nazi Holocaust*. Minneapolis: Lerner Publications, 2000.

Wiesel, Elie. *Night*. Translated by Marion Wiesel. New York: Hill and Wang, 2006.

Study Guide

TO STUDENTS

There are millions of Holocaust stories, each uniquely painful. Kurt and Sonja Messerschmidt tell us one story about their Holocaust. To learn about the Holocaust, this book alone is not enough. But it is an important start. This study guide will help you move from their personal experiences to a broader understanding of the Holocaust.

I hope you will be able to answer factual questions about the Holocaust after you read this book. I have prepared a different set of questions, questions for you to ask of the text as you read these chapters. What Kurt and Sonja describe is so far removed from our normal lives that we have trouble imagining it. Read these questions before you read each chapter, then keep them in mind as you read.

For each chapter

What actions did Kurt and Sonja take to try to save their lives?

Berlin

What could Kurt and Sonja know about what was happening to them at various times?

Make a timeline of what happened to Kurt and Sonja in Berlin. Pick out a minimum of 10 events from this chapter, figure out when they happened, and put them in order. They may not be discussed by Kurt and Sonja in the order in which they happened.

Theresienstadt

What were the Nazis trying to accomplish at Theresienstadt?

Auschwitz

How did the camp work? What processes did Sonja and Kurt undergo?

Why did they survive Auschwitz, when so many more died there? We can't answer that question with any certainty, except to say that luck played an enormous role. But it is useful to think about what they did to increase their chances of survival. What choices did they make about how to prevent the Nazis from killing them?

Slave Labor

Did the use of slave labor help the Nazi war effort?

Death March

Why did the Nazis organize death marches? Again, we cannot know exactly what the Nazi leaders were thinking, but we can try to imagine their motivations.

Liberation

Did liberation from the Nazis mean that the threat of death was gone? Could life go back to normal?

Munich and Maine

Now that Kurt and Sonja had some control over their own lives again, what did they choose to do?

After you finish reading, think about the following broad questions.

What does resistance mean?
Some examples of resistance are obvious: fighting against the Nazis with weapons, as in the Warsaw Ghetto Uprising and the Sobibor revolt and escape. The French who fought a guerilla war against the German occupation called themselves "the Resistance." They sabotaged railroad tracks and the electric power grid, published underground newspapers, and helped Allied airmen trapped behind German lines.

Resistance could be hidden: secretly educating children when that was forbid-den; hiding records of Nazi atrocities for an unknown future. How about trying to save Jews from deportation and death?

Find examples of resistance in *Death and Love*, thinking about both Jewish and non-Jewish actions.

What difference did faith make in the survival of Kurt or Sonja? What differ-ence did love make?

Understanding the Holocaust means knowing what key words mean. You should be able to say a few things about each of these Holocaust words:

Auschwitz
death march
slave labor
extermination camps
displaced persons

Here is a list of more specific words that you should be able to define:

factory action (*Fabrikaktion*)
Gestapo
Kindertransport
Buchenwald
Kristallnacht

Now I pose the question most important to me. As I taught, I sensed the stu-dents and I all believed this course should have some impact on their thinking, on their lives, unlike almost any other course. When I taught a class of students about the Holocaust, I constantly wondered, "What are they taking away?"

Think about that now. What do you want to take away from the horrible things you have learned? How will you think in the future about the beautiful things that so rarely break through into the historical record? Ask yourself, "How do I think about death and love and life from now on?" What difference did this course make?

Index

CPSIA information can be obtained
at www.ICGtesting.com
Printed in the USA
JSHW040725020122
21687JS00001B/1

9 781644 696941